Private Vouchers

The Hoover Institution wishes to acknowledge with gratitude the generous contribution of the William H. Donner Foundation, Inc., for its support of this volume and the Symposium on the Feasibility and Impact of Private Vouchers, held at the Hoover Institution on December 13, 1994.

The papers included here are drawn from those presented at the symposium. The aim of the conference, organized by Senior Fellow Terry M. Moe, was to bring together scholars from around the nation who were doing research on the topic of private vouchers so that they might exchange ideas, learn about one another's work, and think collectively about their future agendas.

This research activity on educational vouchers is one of many projects falling within the Hoover Institution's Program on American Institutions and Economic Performance.

Private Vouchers

Edited by TERRY M. MOE

HOOVER INSTITUTION PRESS
Stanford University
Stanford, California

Hoover Institution Press Publication No. 429

Copyright © 1995 by the Board of Trustees of the
    Leland Stanford Junior University

First printing, 1995
01   00   99   98   97   96   95   9   8   7   6   5   4   3   2   1

Manufactured in the United States of America
⊗ The paper used in this publication meets the minimum requirements
of American National Standard for Information Sciences—Permanence
of Paper for Printed Library Materials, ANSI Z39.48–1984.

Library of Congress Cataloging-in-Publication Data
Private vouchers / edited by Terry M. Moe.
        p.   cm. — (Hoover Institution Press publication : 429)
    Includes bibliographical references.
    ISBN 0-8179-9372-X (alk. paper)
1. Educational vouchers—United States.   2. School choice—United
States.   I. Moe, Terry M.   II. Series.
LB2828.7.P75   1995
379.1′1—dc20   95-37414
                                                           CIP

Contents

Contributors   vii

1   PRIVATE VOUCHERS   1
   Terry M. Moe

2   PRIVATE VOUCHERS IN MILWAUKEE:
   THE PAVE PROGRAM   41
   Janet R. Beales and Maureen Wahl

3   PRIVATE VOUCHERS IN SAN ANTONIO:
   THE CEO PROGRAM   74
   Valerie Martinez, Kenneth Godwin,
   and Frank R. Kemerer

4   PRIVATE VOUCHERS IN INDIANAPOLIS:
   THE GOLDEN RULE PROGRAM   100
   Michael Heise, Kenneth D. Colburn Jr.,
   and Joseph F. Lamberti

5   PRIVATE VOUCHERS IN NEW YORK CITY:
   THE STUDENT-SPONSOR PARTNERSHIP PROGRAM   120
   Paul T. Hill

Contributors

JANET R. BEALES directs the Education Studies Program of the Los Angeles–based Reason Foundation. She holds an MBA degree from the University of Washington and is the author of numerous policy studies and book chapters about education reform. Beales was assistant editor of the *Fortune Encyclopedia of Economics* and a project manager for the U.S. Chamber of Commerce in Washington, D.C. The Reason Foundation is a nonprofit research organization dedicated to finding market-based solutions to public policy issues.

KENNETH D. COLBURN JR. is chairperson and associate professor in the Department of Sociology at Butler University in Indianapolis, Indiana. He received his M.A. and Ph.D. from York University in Toronto, Ontario, Canada. Colburn is interested in the theoretical understanding of postmodern culture and has published papers in the sociology of art, interpersonal violence in sport, and family and gender issues. Of special concern to him is the relationship between the individual and the sociocultural order and the implications of the latter for both social theory and social policy.

KENNETH GODWIN received his Ph.D. from the University of North Carolina in 1972. He is currently a professor of political science at the University of North Texas. His field of expertise is public policy; his recent publications deal with comparing the effectiveness of private and public provision of health care. Godwin was previously a member of the faculties of the Universities of Arizona and

Oregon State. He has also been a senior fellow at Resources for the Future and the Battelle Memorial Institute. Godwin is the author or coauthor of six scholarly books and more than forty published articles and chapters in the field of economics and political science. His research interests are policy evaluation and interest group politics.

MICHAEL HEISE is an assistant professor of law and director of the Program in Law and Education at the Indiana University School of Law in Indianapolis. He is a graduate of Stanford University (A.B., 1983), the University of Chicago Law School (J.D., 1987), and Northwestern University (Ph.D., 1990).

PAUL T. HILL is a research professor in the University of Washington's School of Public Affairs and a senior social scientist with the Rand Corporation. He directs the Program on Reinventing Public Education, a partnership between Rand and the University of Washington's Institute for Public Policy and Management. Hill's recent work has focused on reform of public elementary and secondary education. In early 1994 he published *Reinventing Public Education,* a book concluding that public schools should be operated by independent organizations under contract with public school boards, rather than by government bureaucracies. He holds a Ph.D. and M.A. from Ohio State University and a B.A. from Seattle University, all in political science.

FRANK R. KEMERER received his Ph.D. from Stanford University in educational administration with a law minor from Stanford Law School in 1975. He is currently Regents Professor of Education Law and Administration in the College of Education at the University of North Texas and directs the Center for the Study of Educational Reform. He was designated a Toulouse Scholar by the university in 1991 in recognition of research and teacher excellence. Kemerer previously served as a senior research associate at the Center for Educational Research at Stanford and as a college administrator at the State University of New York, where he also taught courses in constitutional law and civil liberties. Kemerer is the author or coauthor of eleven books in the legal and educational fields and more than forty published articles, book chapters, and research reports.

JOSEPH F. LAMBERTI received his Ed.D. degree from the University of Florida and is a professor of education at Butler University in Indianapolis, Indiana. He has written widely in the field of education and is a member of the board of directors of the American Association of Colleges for Teacher Education and president of the Association of Independent and Liberal Arts College for Teacher Education.

VALERIE MARTINEZ received her Ph.D. from Ohio State University in 1990. She is an assistant professor of political science and a research associate in the Center for the Study of Educational Reform at the University of North Texas, specializing in public policy analysis, program evaluation, and survey research. Her major research interests focus on social welfare policies for children and the elderly. She is principal investigator of an ongoing study, funded by the U.S. Department of Education, which examines the consequences of educational choice policy for low-income minority families in San Antonio.

TERRY M. MOE is a senior fellow at the Hoover Institution and a professor of political science at Stanford University, where he has been on the faculty since 1981. He has also taught at Michigan State University and has served as a senior fellow at the Brookings Institution in Washington, D.C. Moe's teaching and research are concerned most generally with American political institutions, and he has written extensively on a variety of topics, among them public bureaucracy, the presidency, interest groups, and the education system. His recent book, *Politics, Markets, and America's Schools* (coauthored with John E. Chubb), has received national attention for its institutional critique of the American school system and its market-based proposal for sweeping institutional change.

MAUREEN WAHL is an account executive and project director for Market Probe, Inc., a full-service research firm in Milwaukee, Wisconsin. She holds a doctorate in urban education from the University of Wisconsin at Milwaukee. Wahl has many years of experience in designing outcome-based research for mental health services and competency-based education.

1

Private Vouchers

TERRY M. MOE

The voucher movement is the most controversial force for change in American education today. What it proposes—that government provide grants to parents who wish to send their children to private schools—may seem simple enough, a matter of expanding opportunities for American families and imposing a healthy competition on public schools. But vouchers have ignited explosive political battles, as powerful defenders of the public system have put up fierce resistance at every turn. Vouchers have also provoked heated intellectual debate, as supporters and opponents have offered conflicting claims about how these reforms would work out in practice.

While all this has been going on, a little-noticed development has been taking place outside the public sector: individual, corporate, and philanthropic contributors in major U.S. cities have begun setting up their own programs to offer private vouchers to the parents of disadvantaged children. Currently seventeen of these programs are up and running, involving more than 6,500 kids, and more programs are in the planning stages (CEO America 1995a). What began only a few years ago as a charitable experiment in educational choice has grown into a full-fledged movement.

The private voucher movement has a direct bearing on both the political and the intellectual dimensions of the voucher controversy. Politically, it adds new force to the larger movement for school choice nationwide—recruiting new activists, mobilizing new constituencies, bringing new pressures to bear. More generally still, the private voucher movement is an aggressive carrier of what deserves to be called the new politics of education: an ongoing political realignment in which the urban poor, joined by conservatives, do battle with their traditional liberal allies, who are committed to defending the existing system.

The private voucher movement is also significant for its scientific and intellectual value. In a nation where political opponents have defeated (with one small exception) every effort to establish public-sector voucher programs—and with them, any possibility of gathering direct evidence on how vouchers might work—the spread of private voucher programs offers a unique opportunity to learn about vouchers through observation, experience, and study.

This book is, to my knowledge, the first book on the subject of private vouchers. Here in the introductory chapter my aim is to put the movement in perspective by pulling together the political and intellectual strands of its story. The remaining four chapters are concerned more specifically with issues of evidence and research and with what these new programs seem to be telling us—so far—about how vouchers actually work out in practice. They are the reports of research teams that have studied the largest, best-established private voucher programs in the nation—in Milwaukee, San Antonio, Indianapolis, and New York. At this writing, their reports offer the most complete, up-to-date evidence available on private voucher programs and the parents, children, and schools that participate in them.

I can only emphasize, as we take a first look at the evidence, that the private voucher movement is a fast-growing phenomenon whose scope, contours, and effects may well look different in just a few years, not to mention ten or twenty. A book of this sort, then, cannot pretend to make a definitive statement that will stand for the ages. It is best viewed as an early and tentative appraisal, one that is much needed, given the social importance of its subject, but whose role is to pave the way for more definitive work in the future.

The Political Setting of Private Vouchers

In some sense, the private voucher movement is purely private. Its foundations are privately organized, its grants are raised from private sources, and its children use these grants to go to private schools. Nonetheless, the best way to gain perspective on this movement is to begin with a closely related development in politics, a development that is perhaps the most symbolic event in the recent history of U.S. education: the adoption of the Milwaukee public voucher program.[1]

Milwaukee is similar to many other U.S. cities. The school-age population is disproportionately poor and minority, and the public school system is not educating them. Most of Milwaukee's children drop out of school before graduating; of the African-American kids who do graduate, the average grade is a D (Milwaukee Public Schools 1993). There is an escape hatch of sorts. A small proportion of low-income kids are bused to suburban schools, pursuant to a desegregation agreement. But the vast majority remain in the inner city, and many parents don't want their kids bused miles away to school anyway. Like parents elsewhere, they want good schools close to home.

In the late 1980s, a group of Milwaukee parents revolted against the school system. Their leader was Polly Williams, a Democratic state legislator, former welfare recipient, and former state campaign director for Jesse Jackson. Williams blasted the Milwaukee public school system for consistently failing to educate low-income kids. She also rejected busing as a solution. Milwaukee's children deserve good schools close to home, she argued, and if they can't get them in the public sector, the government ought to give them vouchers to help them find better alternatives in the private sector.

Polly Williams's call for vouchers met with an enthusiastic response from Milwaukee's parents. But the usual allies of low-income and minority constituents—Democratic politicians, the educational establishment, and groups like the National Association for the Advancement of Colored People (NAACP)—were vehemently opposed to vouchers, which they saw as an attack on the public school system. So Williams had to look elsewhere for support, and she found it on the other side of the political fence, where Republicans, conservatives, and business groups agreed to back her cause.

After a brutal, closely fought battle, the Williams-led coalition eventually created the nation's first voucher program. Its victory, however, was hedged about by debilitating, if unavoidable, compromises with the other side. It was only a pilot program, limited to a maximum of 1,000 low-income students (in a district of 100,000) and to a set of participating private schools that was guaranteed, by virtue of the program's rules and disincentives, to be exceedingly small. A mere seven participated in the first year, and they did not have anywhere near 1,000 slots for voucher students (Witte 1991).

The Milwaukee design, heavily shaped by the program's enemies, guaranteed that the years ahead would be difficult. But they were also difficult because those same opponents—including the State Department of Public Instruction, which is officially in charge of the program—continued to erect obstacles to its success. Among other things, they challenged its legality all the way to the Wisconsin Supreme Court (where they lost, after imposing almost two years of uncertainty on the program and its participants); they promulgated unfavorable rulings (e.g., turning away schools that wanted to participate); and they failed to publicize the program adequately to parents (McGroarty 1994; Peterson 1994; Bolick 1992). For both sides, the battle continues. At this writing, Governor Tommy Thompson (a Republican) and Polly Williams have gained legislative approval for a big extension of the program, which would dramatically raise the ceiling on how many kids can participate and, for the first time, include religious schools. The education establishment, which fought furiously to defeat the extension, immediately challenged its constitutionality in court, where a temporary injunction was granted. Some observers are now betting that this conflict will lead to the first major ruling by the U.S. Supreme Court on the constitutionality of vouchers (Walsh 1995).

The Milwaukee case speaks volumes about the politics of vouchers and school choice. For anyone interested in the private voucher movement, there is much here to be learned.

CHOICE AND ITS SUPPORTERS

Vouchers were first proposed in the late 1950s by Milton Friedman (1955, 1962), a libertarian economist, and in the last decade, choice of various kinds has been actively supported by conservatives, Republicans, the religious right, and the Reagan administration. So a common stereotype today, not surprisingly, is that these groups provide the bedrock of political support for school choice (Cookson 1994).

There is some truth to this, of course, but the stereotype is misleading. The fact is that poor and minority people are among the strongest supporters of vouchers and choice. More generally, support for choice is *negatively* related to income and education, and its relationship to race is precisely the *opposite* of what conventional wisdom maintains (see, e.g., Coleman et al. 1993; Lee et al. 1994; Cobb, 1992). In the 1992 Gallup poll, for instance, the concept of vouchers was supported by 70 percent of Americans overall but by 85 percent of African Americans and 84 percent of Hispanics.[2] Similar patterns, on a variety of choice-related issues, have been borne out in a large number of national, state, and local polls over the past decade or so. The flip side is that choice receives its weakest support (often outright opposition) from older, well-to-do whites in the suburbs (U. S. Department of Education 1992).

This makes sense. White suburbanites already have choice, which they exercise by buying houses in the best school districts they can find. They are not a natural constituency for vouchers and indeed are often fearful of change. Poor and minority populations in the inner cities, in contrast, tend to be trapped in the nation's worst schools—trapped because, for financial reasons, they have no choice. They want the kind of choice suburbanites already have, and they see vouchers and other choice-based reforms as instrumental to that end.

It is no accident, in view of this, that the first voucher program was for poor kids in Milwaukee, not for upper-middle-class kids in Palo Alto. Similarly, it is no accident that the most highly touted system of public school choice is to be found in East Harlem, where virtually all children are low income and minority.

As a general matter, the choice movement's most dramatic achievements around the nation have occurred in urban areas with high concentrations of poor and minority people—not in suburbia and not in domains controlled by Republicans and conservatives, as the stereotype would suggest (e.g., Nathan 1989; Fliegel and Macquire 1994; Young and Clinchy 1992).

CHOICE AND THE NEW POLITICS OF EDUCATION

On school choice, a deep chasm separates poor people from the politicians and groups that normally represent them. This is not due to ill intentions or bad faith on anyone's part. It is simply inherent in the structure of things, in fundamental interests, beliefs, and incentives that are deeply rooted and difficult to change.

The educational establishment is solidly behind the poor when it comes to mainstream educational programs—for compensatory, bilingual, and special education, for instance. But the establishment has its own reasons for opposing vouchers, even when poor kids are the only ones to receive them. Vouchers allow children and resources to leave the public system. A fully developed voucher system, moreover, would largely dismantle the establishment's own system of bureaucracy and political control in favor of new arrangements that decentralize power to parents and schools. From the establishment's standpoint, then, vouchers are the ultimate survival issue, and they must be defeated wherever they are proposed.

Democratic politicians tend to be strong allies of the poor on social issues. But school choice is a glaring exception, and the educational establishment plays an important role in this. Led by the teachers' unions, they contribute enormous amounts of money and manpower to political campaigns, almost all of it to Democrats. Democrats, in turn, work closely with members of the establishment on educational policy issues—which entails, among other things, opposing vouchers. Some Democrats have broken ranks, and more may follow someday. But for now it is virtually a united front (Lieberman 1993).

Liberal interest groups also weigh into the equation against vouchers. In general, they distrust markets and have agendas that call for extensive government regulation, so vouchers tend to conflict with their basic beliefs and issue positions. The most active in school choice battles is the NAACP. Its present leaders came of age during the civil rights struggles of the 1960s, and their views on school choice are a product of those times. To them, choice is a thinly disguised strategy by which whites seek to avoid integration. This was often accurate decades ago, especially in the South. But times have changed. Now, school choice is regularly relied on to promote integration, while busing and other coercive tools are increasingly out of favor. Indeed, some of the most comprehensive systems of public school choice—in Cambridge, Montclaire, and Kansas City, for example—have evolved in response to desegregation concerns (Nathan 1989; Young and Clinchy 1992).

Be this as it may, the bottom line is that, whereas poor people are highly supportive of school choice, their traditional allies are staunchly opposed, and the divide that separates them will not be bridged in the near future. For those among the poor who want choice, the only recourse in the near term is to find new allies—as Polly Williams did, by entering into coalitions with groups they have traditionally viewed as opponents: Republicans, conservatives, business. This will not happen automatically. The poor are reluctant to trust the motives of their newfound friends. And Republican politicians, who must ultimately push for new laws on their behalf, may often have little incentive to do so, for their own constituencies are typically not pressuring them to move in this direction and may actually be opposed.

Obstacles notwithstanding, this unorthodox alliance is the wave of the future in the politics of school choice. It is already visible and gaining in power and not just in Milwaukee. During the summer of 1995, the Ohio legislature voted to set up a low-income voucher program in Cleveland—which, if the establishment doesn't strike it down somehow, will become the nation's second such program in 1996–97. The coalition behind it was a mirror image of the one that made vouchers a reality in Milwaukee: the grassroots movement was led by Cleveland councilwoman Fannie Lewis—a black Democrat who is that city's Polly Williams—and received critical support from Republicans, particularly Governor George Voinovich. Another key battle over school choice is being fought in Jersey City, where the political coalition is much the same. Here, poor people are finding their educational champion in Brett Schundler who, as a white Republican in an overwhelmingly black Democratic town, was elected mayor on a platform of bringing vouchers to inner-city parents. With Republicans now controlling the governorship and legislature, Schundler and his unorthodox alliance stand a chance of succeeding over the intense opposition of the teachers' unions, Democrats, and liberal interest groups.

Whoever wins, the political battles will continue, and, at least for the foreseeable future, they will take the same coalitional form. This is the new politics of education.

CHOICE, POWER, AND THE STATUS QUO

In Milwaukee, Cleveland, and Jersey City, the choice issue has gotten away from the educational establishment. But this is not the norm. In U.S. education (as in most areas of U.S. public policy, for that matter), the established interests have far more political power than anyone else on issues within their domain. They are extremely well organized, loaded with political resources, and fully focused on education, whose details they follow with tireless determination in every nook and cranny of the political process. The norm is that the establishment dominates the politics of education.

From this flow two basic facts of political life. The first is that, if the establishment is dead set against something, it has little chance of being adopted, at least in the near term. In this sense, Milwaukee is an aberration: one district out of some fifteen thousand in the nation where the establishment's hammerlock was partially broken. As a rule, though, anyone proposing vouchers is likely to lose in today's politics. More generally, choice proposals that represent coherent, far-reaching plans for transforming the system are likely to be threatening to the establishment, powerfully opposed by it, and defeated.

The second is that, when choice-based reforms actually get adopted, they tend to be limited. Although often touted as revolutionary, they are in fact incremental changes that, of political necessity, are simply grafted onto the existing system without altering its fundamentals. Bureaucratic and political control structures remain firmly in place, as does the operational power of the establishment (Lieberman 1993). The programs themselves, moreover, are usually not designed according to the best ideas available. They are political concoctions, built up through a patchwork of compromises as a result of which the establishment has a heavy hand in designing and later operating the very programs it opposes. The Milwaukee voucher program is a case in point. It is a symbol of revolution that is in fact a troubled program: severely limited in scope, hobbled by purposely contrived design restrictions, and subordinated to an official power structure that wants it to fail.[3]

Expectations have to be anchored in the realities of politics. Whatever reforms poor and minority people might favor, the reforms they actually get—if any—will be heavily shaped by establishment interests, submerged in the established system, and so burdened with constraints and official opposition that it is difficult for them to function well. They may signal the beginning of a great transformation. But for now, they are incremental changes, fighting a battle against great odds.

The Emergence of Private Voucher Programs

The private voucher movement is in part a straightforward exercise in philanthropy, and not a new one at that. There is nothing new about the idea of giving low-income children private vouchers. This is just a fancier, more politically charged way of saying that they should be given financial assistance, or scholarships, so that they can attend the private schools of their choice.

It has long been the norm for private schools of all types to have scholarship funds for low-income kids. In most private schools, some percentage of students are attending with the help of what amount to private vouchers. In addition, various foundations around the country, many in urban areas and affiliated with the Catholic Church, provide thousands of needy kids with education grants every year. The Inner-City Scholarship Fund, for instance, provided scholarships to some 2,500 low-income children for the 1992–93 school year, enabling them to attend Catholic schools in the Boston area. Similarly, the archdiocese of the Los Angeles Education Foundation gave out grants in 1992–93 to 3,500 low-income kids who sought to attend Catholic schools in that city (National Scholarship Center 1994).

The private voucher movement, however, goes well beyond these sorts of purely philanthropic efforts.[4] It is in important respects a political as well as a philanthropic movement, and any attempt to understand why it emerged when it did, why it is gaining support and influence, and what consequences it may hold for the future must begin by recognizing its integral connection to the politics of U.S. education.

The leading figures of the private voucher movement—people like J. Patrick Rooney, James Leininger, and Michael Joyce—share a common vision that is a reflection of the political picture I sketched out in the previous section. They believe that the public school system is failing to provide poor children with anything like an adequate education and that bold, innovative steps need to be taken—now—to bring about change for the better. They also believe that school choice, in one form or another, is the key to doing this, and they see themselves as part of the larger choice movement for fundamental reform of the entire system.[5]

They are well aware, however, of the political facts of life. They know that, given the intense opposition to choice among the poor's traditional allies, getting coherent choice plans through the political process is extraordinarily difficult and that any "victories" are likely to take the form of weak, poorly designed compromises that fail to address the urgent needs of low-income students.

The bottom line is that, if they want to help disadvantaged children, and if they want to avoid, as far as possible, the dangers and defeats of the political battlefield, their options are limited. Their resort to privately funded vouchers is essentially an adaptation to political reality.

With private vouchers, they are in a position to bring about immediate change and on their own terms. Assuming enough money can be raised, they can simply design coherent programs according to the best ideas available and put them into effect quickly and with a maximum of flexibility. Low-income children get the benefits right away, and private schools are able to participate without debilitating regulatory burdens. Meantime, opponents cannot block, subvert, delay, oversee, or impose restrictions.

There is, however, one obvious drawback. The educational problems facing the entire population of low-income children are simply too overwhelming to be solved through private contributions. There is literally no way that privately funded voucher programs could extend to millions of kids. In the end, if vouchers are to bring improvements on a large scale, they must be publicly funded: the government must use tax money to finance a new system of school choice. And this runs into the same political buzz saw that has plagued vouchers from the outset.

Taking this as a given, however, leaders see a second advantage in the private voucher approach: it is an innovative way of pressing for permanent, broadly based changes in the educational system without becoming immersed in politics. The idea is that private voucher programs will serve as models for reform. Objectively, these programs would provide policy makers with a much-needed storehouse of direct evidence that, outside of Milwaukee's public voucher system, is lacking in the debate over vouchers. The expectation is that they would demonstrate through actual practice that vouchers can indeed enhance opportunities for low-income kids—thereby influencing the public debate and turning public and elite opinion in favor of vouchers. Along the way, low-income constituencies in urban areas would get mobilized, bring pressure to bear on their representatives, and create a more favorable political setting.

As all this suggests, the private voucher movement is part philanthropy, part political reform. As philanthropy, it is not so different from other charitable programs, run by individual private schools and foundations, that give educational scholarships to low-income children. The political dimension is what makes it different and lends it much broader national significance.

THE GOLDEN RULE MODEL

Most activists within the private voucher movement would point to one man as its founder and guiding spirit: J. Patrick Rooney, chief executive officer of the Golden Rule Insurance Company. In August 1991, following the defeat of a voucher proposal in the Indiana state legislature, Rooney announced the creation of the Educational Choice Charitable Trust, a private foundation whose purpose was to provide financial assistance—private vouchers—to low-income children within the Indianapolis public school system.[6]

In principle, there are many ways to design a private voucher scheme. Rooney chose to build his Golden Rule program around the following basic elements:

1. Vouchers would be equal to half the receiving private school's tuition, subject to some ceiling amount, with parents responsible for paying or raising the remainder.

2. Only low-income children would be eligible. This includes low-income children already attending private schools.

3. Families would be allowed to use vouchers at whatever private schools they wanted, whether independent or religious.

4. Low-income children would be granted vouchers on a first-come, first-served basis. There would be no requirements, academic or otherwise, aside from the admissions standards of the specific schools they choose to attend.

The first is perhaps the most pivotal and defining component of the Golden Rule model: parents can get vouchers only if they are committed enough to contribute half the tuition out of their own resources. This is useful as a practical matter because it essentially doubles the number of parents and children the program can reach, compared with a system in which vouchers cover all tuition costs. But it is also rooted in a fundamental principle that guides Rooney's thinking: If parents become financial stakeholders in their children's educations, they are likely to be more involved and take it more seriously and their children are likely to gain more from the experience. The financial burden this entails, moreover, is not great because the tuition at most Indianapolis private schools is low to begin with, often close to $1,000.

The second element of the Golden Rule model ensures that vouchers will go not only to low-income children who want to avoid or leave the public schools but also to those who are already attending private schools—and whose parents, therefore, have already found a way to pay for these schools. The idea is that poor parents who are struggling to pay full tuition for their children should not be penalized for their motivation, commitment, and sacrifice; the program is designed to support those parents' efforts to keep their children in the private schools of their choice. The downside is that less program money is available to support children who are trapped in inadequate public schools, which is presumably the more salient problem. Rooney's solution has been to compromise. In practice, the Golden Rule program has allotted about half its vouchers over the past few years to children who are already in private schools, the other half to children who are not.

The model's third element gives families complete freedom to choose whichever school they want, including religious schools. This maximizes the chances that parents will find schools with the desirable properties they are looking for and that match up well with their children's needs. The inclusion of religious schools is a crucial part of this. Many parents value the discipline, moral climate, and academic rigor of religious schools. Moreover, the vast majority of private schools, in Indianapolis and throughout the country, are religiously affiliated. Any system of educational choice or vouchers that excludes religious schools, then, not only would prevent many parents from choosing the schools they want, it would drastically reduce the supply of participating schools and fail to take advantage of the diversity, dynamism, and resources the private sector has to offer.

The fourth element is intended to ensure that all low-income children are eligible for vouchers on an equal basis. Rooney's mechanism for assuring equal treatment is first-come, first-served: children receive priority based on when their applications are received, not on the basis of their aptitude, grades, behavior, or personal connections. There are, of course, implicit criteria at work here, namely, those of the receiving schools. But their standards are presumably accepted by the parents who choose them and, outside of a small number of elite schools, can readily be met by a broad cross section of children. This is particularly true of religious schools, which are not only quite numerous but actively concerned with aiding needy children (National Catholic Educational Association 1985; Coleman and Hoffer 1987; Bryk et al. 1993).

Rooney's announcement of the Golden Rule voucher program, which was publicized in the media as well as through various church, school, and community networks, produced an overwhelming response from poor parents. Initially, his plan was to create a three-year program capable of funding five hundred students a year. But within three days of his announcement, more than six hundred applications had come in, followed thereafter by some nine hundred more (Beales 1994). Right away, then, his program was hugely oversubscribed, suggesting that Rooney was onto something: there did indeed appear to be a pent-up demand among the poor for educational choice, and many were eager to take advantage of vouchers even when asked to shoulder some of the financial burden themselves.

Rooney responded,with the help of Eli Lilly and scores of other new contributors, by raising additional funds and expanding the scope of the progam. During the first year, vouchers were given out to 744 children instead of the planned 500. The numbers increased to around 900 in 1992–93 and 1,100 in 1993–94. The three-year time horizon was extended to five, with the understanding that, if more contributions could be raised, the program would likely be continued beyond that. What began as a novel, short-term experiment rather quickly showed signs of developing into something of an institution (National Scholarship Center 1994).

In the meantime, the innovative example and early success of the Golden Rule program—publicized through the national media, as well as through countless speeches given by Rooney and Tim Ehrgott, Golden Rule's administrator, as part of a consciously orchestrated outreach effort—attracted attention from potential organizers, contributors, and supporters in cities all around the country. The result, in very short order, was a proliferation of new private voucher programs and the emergence of a movement truly national in scope.

REPLICATING THE GOLDEN RULE MODEL

At this writing, the two largest private voucher programs inspired by the Golden Rule experience are located in Milwaukee and San Antonio. Both began operation with the 1992–93 school year, just one year after Rooney's initial announcement, and both were explicitly designed in accordance with the Golden Rule model.

The San Antonio program grew out of the leadership of James Leininger, CEO of Kinetic Concepts, a medical supply company, and chairman of the Texas Public Policy Foundation, a conservative policy organization.[7] Leininger first got excited about the idea of private vouchers when he read a *Wall Street Journal* article on Rooney and Golden Rule, and he soon resolved to create such a program for San Antonio, an overwhelmingly Hispanic city in which the vast majority of families are low income.

Leininger enlisted the support of Jack Antonini, president of the USAA Federal Savings Bank, and Larry Walker, publisher of the San Antonio *Express-News*, among others. Under the auspices of the Texas Public Policy Foundation, they set up the Children's Educational Opportunity (CEO) Foundation and endowed it with a $1.5 million fund for private vouchers. The *Express-News* pitched in to publicize the new program, and San Antonio's low-income families responded with an enthusiasm that paralleled the Golden Rule experience. The CEO program was announced in April of 1992, and by September it was flooded with some 2,200 applications, far more than could be funded (Martinez et al. 1995).

For the 1993–94 school year, close to 950 children were granted educational vouchers averaging about $550 a child—which, again, was generally half the receiving school's tuition in a city where the average private school charged about $1,100 per year (Beales 1994). Since then, the size of the program has stayed roughly the same. Demand among San Antonio's poor, meantime, has continued to far outstrip the program's capacity, and the waiting list remains long.

The Milwaukee private voucher program is the largest in the country and is currently much larger than the ones in San Antonio and Indianapolis.[8] One reason, almost surely, is that it was not built from scratch, as they were, through newly mobilized resources and newly formed organizations. Rather, the Milwaukee program arose from an institutional base, the Milwaukee Archdiocesan Education Foundation, that had been set up earlier to provide aid to children and Catholic schools in the inner city.

The foundation sought to address the growing crisis that afflicts not only Milwaukee Catholic schools but urban Catholic schools throughout the nation: as whites and the more affluent have fled to the suburbs, inner-city Catholic schools have been left with fewer resources and a population of low-income minority students whose families cannot afford the schools' services. The church sees its social mission as one of helping these children, most of whom are non-

Catholic, but pursuing this mission requires resources that neither the church nor its client families can muster. As a result, Catholic schools have been closing in record numbers around the country (National Catholic Educational Association 1985).

A prime goal of the Milwaukee Archdiocesan Education Foundation was to see that this did not happen in Milwaukee. Initially, it sought to create a coalition of supporters, many of them from the business community, to provide financial aid to the city's Catholic schools and the inner-city children who attend them. In 1990, the foundation formed a more broadly based coalition—representing the full range of private schools in the city, religious and nonreligious, Catholic and non-Catholic—for the purpose of raising funds to support private education and low-income students in Milwaukee.

In the midst of this campaign, Patrick Rooney announced the Golden Rule program, which quickly emerged as a focal point for the Milwaukee coalition. The foundation then contributed its $800,000 trust toward the creation of a new private voucher program—known as Partners Advancing Values in Education (PAVE)—modeled along the lines of Golden Rule. The Bradley Foundation, under the leadership of Michael Joyce, assumed a central role in the new PAVE program and pledged another $500,000 a year for three years. Other foundations and businesses, many of them already part of the archdiocese's network of supporters, joined in with major contributions.

The PAVE experience has been much the same as those of Golden Rule and CEO but on a grander scale. From the beginning, it was overwhelmed with applications from low-income families, as were the other programs, but its extensive funding base allowed it to provide many more of them with vouchers. During its first year of operation, 1992–93, it funded 2,089 children, and over the next few years it added about 500 more—making it larger than Golden Rule and CEO combined. Currently, there are another 2,000 Milwaukee children on the waiting list hoping to get vouchers (Beales 1994; O'Malley and Associates 1994). Although the initial plan was for three years, PAVE's leaders have responded to the early enthusiasm by mobilizing new resources and extending the program's time horizon, as their colleagues did in Indianapolis and San Antonio.

What makes the PAVE program unique is that it operates in the same city as the nation's only public voucher system. While Polly Williams's public program has attracted widespread national attention, PAVE has quietly been handing out more than three times as many vouchers to Milwaukee schoolchildren every year, dwarfing the public program in scope and impact. Moreover, although social scientists and educators have looked solely to the public program as the source of new data on the impact of vouchers, PAVE clearly represents a data source of major importance—because of its size, because of the obvious opportunities for fruitful comparisons to the public program, and, not least, because PAVE (like

Table 1   Enrollments in Golden Rule–Type Programs

	NUMBER OF CHILDREN			
City	1991–92	1992–93	1993–94	1994–95
Albany	—	—	24	24
Atlanta	—	200	163	162
Austin	—	—	46	69
Battle Creek, Michigan	—	53	116	180
Dallas	—	—	—	100
Denver	—	—	39	78
Detroit/Grand Rapids	—	—	8	13
Houston	—	—	—	100
Indianapolis	744	900	1,100	1,100
Little Rock	—	—	17	17
Los Angeles	—	—	—	775
Midland, Texas	—	—	—	8
Milwaukee	—	2,089	2,450	2,650
Oakland	—	—	—	161
Phoenix	—	—	60	60
San Antonio	—	930	950	900
Washington, D.C.	—	—	50	175
TOTALS	744	4,172	5,023	6,572

* Data for the 1991–92, 1992–93, and 1993–94 school years are from the National Scholarship Center 1994. Data for the 1994–95 school year are from CEO America 1995a.

its sister programs) is not encumbered by the debilitating design restrictions that distort the operation of vouchers in the public program.

GROWTH AND INSTITUTIONALIZATION: 1991–1995

With Golden Rule as a model, the private voucher movement took off (see table 1). The 1992–93 school year saw new programs up and running in Milwaukee, San Antonio, Battle Creek, and Atlanta. Seven additional cities—Albany, Austin, Denver, Detroit/Grand Rapids, Phoenix, Little Rock, and Washington, D.C.—joined the list in 1993–94. In 1994–95, there was another surge of new programs, with organizations sprouting up in Los Angeles, Oakland, Houston, Dallas, and Midland, Texas. At this writing, still more are on the drawing boards in some thirty other cities (CEO America 1995b).

There are now more than 6,500 children receiving private vouchers under Golden Rule–type programs, and almost twice that many are on the waiting list (CEO America 1995a).[9] There is considerable variation, however, in the size of these programs across cities. The Los Angeles organization, spearheaded by John Walton (of Wal-Mart) and Larry Smead (of SASCO Electric), has put together the only new program that currently rivals those in Indianapolis, San Antonio, and Milwaukee, giving out 775 vouchers in its first year of operation, 1994–95. All the other voucher programs are much smaller than the big four, enrolling fewer than two hundred children each—although most of these programs are growing.

There is a rationale to this, of course. The proliferation of small programs gives the Golden Rule model a concrete presence in cities throughout the nation; they serve as pilot programs to demonstrate the value of vouchers; they provide a propitious and necessary basis for future growth; and they help people who need it. But the sheer number of cities involved is a misleading indicator of the population of children able to participate. Of the more than 6,500 children currently receiving private vouchers under the Golden Rule model, some 5,400 of them live in Indianapolis, San Antonio, Milwaukee, or Los Angeles.

As with most movements, the spread of private voucher programs has largely been driven by spontaneous action on the part of activists seeking to pioneer change in their own cities. From the beginning, however, certain individuals have taken on larger leadership roles—promoting the cause, stimulating the emergence of programs across cities, assisting with funding, coordinating far-flung people and activities—with considerable influence on the rapid growth and increasing coherence of the movement as a whole. Patrick Rooney did exactly these sorts of things in his attempts to launch the movement on a nationwide basis and get it established. Once begun, others played leading roles on a national scale as well. Michael Joyce and the Bradley Foundation stand out in this regard; they not only helped fund and organize the huge Milwaukee program but also played an active part in publicizing and promoting the movement nationally.

It is the San Antonio group, however, acting through the Texas Public Policy Foundation, that has done the most to lay an organizational foundation for central leadership and to institutionalize the movement. Aided by a grant from the Famsea Corporation in late 1992, it fashioned a campaign to stimulate interest in private vouchers and assist local activists in setting up their own programs, providing, among other things, a two hundred-page how-to manual offering step-by-step guidance. It also launched a comprehensive outreach effort—involving networking and travel by San Antonio activists, videotapes, brochures, and a national conference—to publicize the CEO experience and spark national interest (CEO America 1994).

In the spring of 1994, with the help of a $2 million grant from the Walton Family Foundation, the San Antonio group followed up with what may turn out to be the most important single development since Rooney created Golden Rule: it set up a new centralizing entity, CEO America, to provide institutional leadership for the movement. CEO America's mission is to serve as a clearinghouse and umbrella organization for all existing private voucher programs and to assist in the creation of new ones. Its assistance involves more than information and advice. CEO America provides challenge grants (on a matching basis) of up to $50,000 to initiate programs in new cities, as well as to stimulate the expansion of smaller existing programs. Translated into practice, these are significant amounts: a challenge grant of $50,000, matched by local donors, is enough to provide vouchers for up to two hundred children (CEO America 1994).

With the emergence of CEO America, the private voucher movement is showing signs of coming of age. Whether it will continue to grow and prosper remains to be seen. But it is no longer an uncoordinated assemblage of activists. It is increasingly a well-organized endeavor with a rationally designed institutional base.

AN ALTERNATIVE MODEL:
THE STUDENT-SPONSOR PARTNERSHIP

As I suggested earlier, the Golden Rule model is just one of many ways to design a private voucher program. Over the last several years, however, it has provided a common conceptual orientation for activists around the country, to the point where the movement is now virtually identified with the model.

Identification with a single model is understandable at this early stage, for, although there have long been private scholarship programs of various sorts (which are little more than private voucher programs under a different name), the idea of private vouchers per se took on intellectual coherence and political force as a direct outgrowth of Golden Rule, which provided a focal point, a rationale, and a concrete example for others to follow. The model gave rise to a movement, and the movement has embraced the model.

Yet the singular influence of Golden Rule will almost surely give way to more pluralistic approaches. Rooney's ideas were pathbreaking and seminal; but there are plenty of new approaches that make good sense as well, and these will be tried out as new people and cities are drawn into the movement and as experience reveals problems and opportunities that argue for innovations in the original model.

A number of existing programs might serve as points of departure in the search for new ideas. But one, in my view, stands out: the Student-Sponsor Partnership (SSP) in New York City.[10] This program was started in 1986—five years before Golden Rule—by Peter Flanigan, an attorney and managing director of Dillon, Read & Company. Flanigan, like Rooney, was critical of the dismal quality of urban public education, and he sought to promote educational opportunity for inner-city kids by helping them attend local Catholic schools. But the program he designed is strikingly different from Golden Rule in key respects.

As the name suggests, the SSP program is built around a partnership between each student and an adult sponsor. Whereas Golden Rule collects money, puts it into a central pot, and distributes it, the SSP program links each child with an adult sponsor who agrees to contribute a certain amount toward that child's tuition and thereafter to serve as a mentor and role model to nurture educational success, high school graduation, and aspirations for college. Most sponsors are under forty, have successful professional careers (many in New York City's financial industry), and are personally committed to the success of the children they sponsor, whom they come to know on a personal basis.

Golden Rule is focused almost solely on elementary school students, who essentially self-select into the program. The Student-Sponsor Partnership targets high school–age students who either are at risk of dropping out or have actually dropped out. And it identifies them not through self-selection but by relying on referrals from teachers, guidance counselors, and community organizations. Of children thus identified, the program then chooses those that it believes are most in need of assistance, rather than simply accepting them on a first-come, first-served basis; it places them in carefully selected Catholic schools that it feels are most appropriate for their needs and interests, rather than leaving the choice of schools up to the family; and it pays the entire tuition bill.

The number of children getting vouchers through the Student-Sponsor Partnership has increased steadily over the years, reaching 821 in 1994–95. These students, virtually all of them from the public schools (or dropped out of public schools), are distributed across fifteen Catholic schools in New York City. The average tuition in these schools is $3,034, much higher than comparable tuitions for the other cities we have looked at but still quite low relative to what is currently spent in the New York City public schools. More than two-thirds of the tuition cost, an average of $2,253, is covered by sponsor contributions, representing a substantial personal investment by each sponsor in a given child's education. The remainder of the tuition cost is covered by the program through additional fund-raising.[11]

In sheer size, then, the New York program rivals those in Indianapolis and San Antonio. It is well established, has a relatively long track record, and offers a design based on a sensible, ethical rationale. Yet, since its inception in 1986, it has not spawned a host of imitators around the country. A few SSP-type programs have emerged in other urban areas, but they are small and, at this point, peripheral to the thrust of the larger private voucher movement, which is clearly coming from the Golden Rule and its energetic proponents.

For SSP, I suspect, this sort of peripheral role is likely to continue, as it is much more difficult to set up a program based on sponsorships and personal mentoring than it is to follow the Golden Rule approach. Nonetheless, there is much to be learned from SSP and other program designs, and I expect that, as the evidence starts to come in and comparisons across programs are made, they will have a marked influence on how future programs are designed and on their consequences for academic achievement and equal opportunity.

Evidence and Politics

The leaders of the private voucher movement are dedicated to fundamental reform of the U.S. school system through vouchers. They believe that their programs, by generating hard evidence that vouchers do work, can inform and shape the public debate, put substantial force behind the arguments for vouchers, and lead the way toward political success in state legislatures around the country.

In the short run at least, this is an optimistic scenario. For even if their programs turn out to be great successes by any objective standard, politics is often unmoved by convincing evidence. Tobacco clearly kills people, but the government still subsidizes its production because tobacco farmers and their legislative representatives are so politically powerful. In politics, it is power that counts. Evidence is essentially a tool, and as power brokers manipulate it to their own advantage, truth gives way to interpretation, nuance, and selective omission (e.g. Edelman 1985; Ornstein and Elder 1978). So even if the evidence seems clear, convincing, and on your side, it may or may not mean much. And it certainly will not change the views of the opposition. In the present case, establishment groups will oppose vouchers no matter what because it is in their best interests to do so.

Still, evidence does matter in politics, especially to the people, groups, and policy makers who are largely uncommitted. Although the educational establishment is usually powerful enough to carry the day on issues that concern it, there are special issues, times, and places when the uncommitteds turn out to be crucial, when evidence really does count, and when radical changes can be brought about because of it. So the private voucher strategy of generating evidence may well pay off. But its successes will occur unpredictably, when the political stars happen to line up just right, and not simply because the empirical case has been made persuasively (Kingdon 1984).

To the extent that evidence does matter to the voucher debate, the private voucher movement is of pivotal importance. For at this point there is little direct evidence of how educational voucher programs actually work in practice. The reason for the lack of evidence is, again, fundamentally political: there can be no evidence without operating voucher programs, but the establishment has used its power to prevent the initiation of such programs, even on a limited and experimental basis—arguing, among other things, that it would be wrong to adopt vouchers in the absence of evidence that they work! This is a catch-22 that the establishment has long played on. But because of the new evidence being generated by the private voucher movement—which does not need establishment consent to carry out its programs—the catch-22 may soon come to an end.

Observations on the Research Literature

Before I summarize what has so far been learned from these new programs, I want to offer some brief observations on the current research literature. Perhaps the most important point to underline is that, because all but one effort to enact a public voucher program has been defeated by the establishment, that single program—the Milwaukee Public Choice Program—has become the focus of extraordinary national attention, as though its performance is the critical test of whether vouchers work. This is unfortunate and potentially misleading.

Voucher programs can be designed in all sorts of different ways, and Milwaukee's design is just one possibility—and a bad one at that. As I suggested earlier, a number of onerous restrictions have been heaped on the program by its political opponents, making it difficult for market forces to work at all. Among other things these restrictions have drastically limited the supply of schools in the program—which limits choice, limits competition, and limits what we can learn about vouchers. Indeed, because just three schools currently enroll more than three-fourths of the children in the program—a stunningly important fact almost everyone seems to ignore—any assessments of performance, attrition, parent satisfaction, and the like turn almost entirely on how those three schools are doing.[12] This is hardly a solid basis for evaluating the effects of vouchers. In fact, it verges on the ridiculous.

The official evaluation of the Milwaukee choice program—carried out by John Witte, who was selected for the job by Wisconsin's Department of Public Instruction—has pointed to mixed results. On performance grounds, voucher parents are more satisfied with their schools than are public school parents, but there is no clear evidence that their children are achieving more academically. On equity grounds, voucher schools are not skimming the best low-income students from the public schools, as critics had feared, and indeed are attracting children who were doing worse in public schools than other low-income kids. Voucher parents, however, have more education than low-income public school parents, higher expectations for their children, and participate more—which is a skimming effect (Witte 1991; Witte et al. 1992, 1993–94).

Witte's net evaluation of the program is modestly positive but highly qualified. Voucher supporters—who do not have direct access to all the data (no one but Witte does)—see it much more favorably and accuse him of emphasizing the negative (McGroarty 1994; Peterson 1995). All the controversy notwithstanding, though, we have to remember that this is a small, highly restricted program that cannot tell us much one way or the other, at least as it is currently constituted.

There is, in addition to Witte's work on Milwaukee, a growing research literature on school choice more generally that mainly consists of two types of studies: studies of public-private differences and studies of public school choice systems (see, e.g., Coleman et al. 1982; Coleman and Hoffer 1987; Chubb and Moe 1990; Cookson 1994; Crain et al. 1992; Clune and Witte 1990; Haertel et al. 1987; Hill et al. 1990; Nathan 1989; Rasell and Rothstein 1993; Wells 1993; Young and Clinchy 1992). The evidence here is less direct, of course, in what it has to say about vouchers. It is sketchy and incomplete on most issues of relevance; it is extraordinarily complicated, due to the great variety of contexts, programs, and variables involved; and its interpretation often seems to be shaped by ideological rather than objective concerns.

Ideology aside, perhaps the most vexing problem is that few researchers who carry out studies of school choice are sensitive to issues of institutional design or context. They proceed as though their case studies reveal something generic about choice or markets when, in fact—as the Milwaukee case graphically testifies—much of what they observe is due to the specific rules, restrictions, and control mechanisms that shape how choice and markets happen to operate in a particular setting. As any economist would be quick to point out, the effects of choice and markets vary, sometimes enormously, depending on the institutional context. The empirical literature on school choice does little to shed light on these contingencies and, indeed, by portraying choice and markets as generic reforms with generic effects, often breeds more confusion than understanding.

Any effort to sort all this out in a balanced, instructive way would require an extensive discussion that would take me far afield. Instead, as I review the recent research on private vouchers in the section below, I will simply try to suggest how it fits with some of the findings and claims that have currency in today's debate over vouchers.

I should add, finally, that the confused state of the research literature only underlines the importance of studying private voucher programs. Their value is not just that they provide additional, much-needed evidence. It is that they allow us to explore how choice and markets tend to work in the absence of most of the rules and restrictions that shape—and often suffocate—the various school choice programs in the public sector. Private voucher programs have their own rules. And these rules, as I will suggest, have a lot to do with the kinds of outcomes that get generated. But in comparison with the public programs, private voucher programs give us a simpler, more direct indication of how choice and markets actually operate when the most burdensome trappings of bureaucracy and political control are removed.

The Early Evidence on Private Vouchers

To the leaders of the private voucher movement, evidence is a key means of influencing public policy; so it only makes sense that each of the major Golden Rule–type programs featured here — Indianapolis, San Antonio, and Milwaukee — has contracted with a research team to collect data, carry out analysis, and publish reports on various aspects of its performance. There is a certain amount of coordination among these groups. (All, for instance, have chosen to survey participating parents by using a common set of items taken from John Witte's study of Milwaukee's public voucher program.) For the most part, however, these are independent outfits that design and carry out their own research in their own ways, so there is not as much comparability as one might like — or might have expected, given its obvious advantages to the movement.

The reality, moreover, is that they are forced to operate on tight budgets, which means that they cannot afford to pursue the kinds of comprehensive, high-tech survey operations they would surely prefer and that many researchers at universities and think tanks have come to expect. The movement's leaders wanted data and evaluation and were willing to invest a certain amount of money to get it, but they were also painfully aware that every dollar spent on research was a dollar that could not go toward a voucher for a needy child. This trade-off proved a major constraint.

New York City's Student-Sponsor Partnership is in a different category when it comes to research. Because it was not conceived as an effort to bring empirical data to bear on public policy, its leaders did not elevate research to a top priority. Unlike the other programs, then, it did not arrange for a research team to collect and analyze data. It does, however, maintain good information on its students and has done a diligent job of tracking them over time. In addition, the SSP was included several years ago in a larger research project on New York City schools carried out by Hill et al. (1993), and Hill, who authors the chapter on SSP in this book, is thus in a good position to offer an informed assessment of its performance.

These departures from the ideal are worth noting. But the point to be emphasized is that we are fortunate to have these data sources at all, that there is a great deal to be learned from them, and that they provide an exciting basis for further work.[13]

SCHOOLS

On the supply side, the Golden Rule–type programs offer a striking contrast to the Milwaukee public choice program. The latter gives students very little choice, and virtually all students end up in just a few schools. Milwaukee's private voucher program, in contrast, allows students to choose whatever schools they want within the private sector as a whole—and when given a free choice, students end up distributing themselves across more than one hundred schools. In Indianapolis, the comparable figure is sixty. This suggests that there is more diversity within the student population than the public program comes close to accommodating and that its restrictions on supply are preventing students from seeking out other schools they would prefer to attend. It also suggests, contrary to the familiar equity arguments of critics (e.g., Cookson 1994; Wells 1993), that large numbers of schools in the private sector are ready and willing to provide spaces for low-income children with vouchers.

The vast majority of voucher students—95 percent in Milwaukee, 99 percent in San Antonio, 80 percent in Indianapolis—choose to attend religious schools of one kind or another. About 60 percent in fact go to Catholic schools. Some observers may be tempted to come up with a conspiracy theory of sorts to explain this, for the key leaders in the movement are themselves Catholics who are personally supportive of religous schools and, from the beginning, have recognized the contribution vouchers can make to the survival and financial well-being of these schools. But this ignores the special role that Catholic schools have long played in helping disadvantaged children and its centrality to their educational mission (e.g., Coleman and Hoffer 1987; Bryk et al. 1993). Moreover, leaders have purposely designed their programs to give students a free choice of schools, and most students have freely chosen to attend religious schools. This is precisely what we should expect to see anyway, given the supply and demand characteristics of today's private marketplace, for the current supply of private schools is overwhelmingly religious.

The current movement of students into religious schools is not necessarily an indication of what would happen in the long run if vouchers were generally available. Although there is a genuine demand for what religious schools are reputed to offer—academic quality in an environment of strong moral values and strict discipline—there is also a demand for nonreligious education. At the present time, however, this demand gives rise to little supply-side response because there exists a secular public school system that is free of charge. Secular private schools cannot easily compete because they are so expensive by comparison (Lieberman 1993). If vouchers were widely available, the price of these schools would be reduced, they would become more attractive as educational alternatives, their supply would increase, and more students would move into them.

The Student-Sponsor Partnership deserves separate treatment because it does not simply give families vouchers and let them choose their own schools. SSP essentially places children in schools that appear appropriate for them, based on the staff's familiarity with the quality, track record, and programmatic offerings of the various schools in the area. As a result its 821 children are bunched in just fifteen schools. The advantage of this strategy—magnified, to some extent, by the information problems currently facing low-income families—is that SSP staff can use the marketplace selectively to ensure that children attend good schools. The downside, administrative costs aside, is that its benevolent central planning gives families less freedom to seek out other schools that may indeed be more appropriate and, over the long haul, gives them little incentive to become more informed. Whether the advantages outweigh the disadvantages is an empirical question, one that comparisons across programs may help to answer.

DEMOGRAPHICS: VOUCHERS AND THE SKIMMING PROBLEM

A standard criticism of school choice is that it leads to social inequities. When families are free to choose, critics argue, the families who are the most highly motivated, well informed, and well-to-do are the ones who are especially likely to take advantage of it. The result is a skimming effect in which choice programs—and private schools, if vouchers are involved—"skim the cream," and less fortunate or capable families are left with less desirable opportunities, and unequal ones (Levin 1989; Kozol 1991; Cookson 1992; Wells 1993a).

There is clearly some merit to this argument (Moe 1995). Skimming is rooted in the calculus of choice itself: in the utility functions of parents, the information they bring to bear, and their income constraints. Some parents put a higher value on education than others and so are willing to give up more to secure quality schooling for their children. Some parents have more information than others and thus know more about what schools are available and how good they are. And some parents have higher incomes than others and so are better able to acquire good information and afford good schools. Unrestricted choice, then, may well lead to selection effects with a class bias.

In practice, I should emphasize, these skimming effects may be mitigated or even reversed by a reality of U.S. social life: the people who are disadvantaged on these decisional grounds also tend to be stuck in the worst schools. They have *more to gain* than their advantaged counterparts do, therefore, in seeking out new opportunities that choice makes available. Nonetheless, taken by themselves, the choice-based factors I just outlined do tend to produce skimming effects, and their potential for doing so is a troublesome (and predictable) problem that needs to be clearly recognized.

It is a mistake, however, to think that skimming is somehow limited to free markets. America's education system today, for instance, is based on top-down political control, bureaucratic management, and student assignment by geographic area, yet it still suffers serious skimming problems. The main culprit is residential mobility; people are free to live where they want, and those who value education highly and have the money to pay for it tend to move to suburban districts with good schools. In urban areas with troubled schools, the only families left are those with too little money to get out. The result is a public education system highly segregated by class and race. This is a skimming effect.

Two points are central to a balanced perspective on vouchers and the skimming problem (Moe 1995). First, the assessment has to be comparative, rather than riveted on vouchers per se. The issue is not whether vouchers totally eliminate all vestiges and types of skimming. The issue is whether they improve on the current system's skimming problem—which is quite bad—or make it worse. Second, the extent of the skimming problem is highly dependent on the setting of rules, constraints, and controls in which choice takes place, and it can be socially engineered through appropriate institutional design. Any choice program, in principle, can be consciously designed to reduce skimming and promote equal opportunity.

With this background, let's consider the demographics of who participates in private voucher programs. If social equity is the primary concern, the place to start is by underlining the most fundamental feature of these programs: they are restricted by design to the most disadvantaged members of society. Not surprisingly, then, compared with the population as a whole, the families who participate are significantly lower in income, more likely to be minorities, less likely to have two parents, and so on than the general population. In this crucial respect, private vouchers clearly strike a blow for social equity. They engage in "reverse skimming," setting up a design in which only the disadvantaged are allowed to reap the benefits of choice.

A rather different picture emerges if we compare program participants not with the population at large but with other low-income families. Here we expect that, in the absence of conscious design efforts to avoid it, the sorts of class-based selection effects I discussed earlier could assert themselves, and that the "most advantaged of the disadvantaged" may be the ones who disproportionately take advantage of private vouchers. And this is pretty much what the data indicate.

The Golden Rule–type programs tend to attract parents who are somewhat more likely to be white, married, and have fewer children than other low-income families and thus to be relatively advantaged in these respects. But the most consequential difference by far is that voucher parents tend to be much better educated than other low-income parents and to have higher expectations for their kids. In San Antonio, for instance, 55 percent of CEO female parents had at least some college, whereas only 19 percent of female public school parents had that much education. The same gap, not surprisingly, applies to educational expectations: 52 percent of CEO parents expect their children to continue education beyond the college level, compared with 17 percent of public school parents.

This is a skimming effect. It is far less important, to be sure, than the programs' larger and positive impact on social equity. But it is still an outcome that many observers would consider undesirable. The better-educated low-income parents, we can presume, place greater emphasis on their children's educations, are more strongly motivated to seek out better schools for them, are better in-formed about private voucher programs and what they offer, and know how to get involved. These qualities give them pivotal advantages over other low-income parents whose children, as a result, do not have an equal opportunity to partici-pate.

It is reasonable to suggest that three elements of the Golden Rule design may be allowing this skimming effect to emerge: (1) that participants are asked to pay half the tuition; (2) that half the vouchers are given out to children already in private schools; and (3) that children are admitted on a first-come, first-served basis. All three may encourage a selection bias favoring the most highly educated, and thus the most highly motivated, parents.

Although it is difficult to tell at this point, data on Milwaukee suggest that the money dimension may not be all that important, at least in this regard; for PAVE parents (who pay half the tuition) and parents in the public voucher program (where tuition is free) have virtually identical educational profiles. The second element may not be important either. Although the practice of reserving half the vouchers for children already in private schools may be objectionable on other grounds, there is no evidence that the skimming effects are due to the higher education levels of these parents alone. As the reports on Milwaukee and Indianapolis indicate, the parents of voucher children previously enrolled in public schools have educational levels that are just as high. This, indeed, is an interesting finding in itself, because it suggests that the latter parents are very much like private school parents in all basic respects except that, in the absence of vouchers, they cannot afford to go private. The nub of the skimming problem, then, may simply be the third element: that children are accepted on a first-come, first-served basis, and under such a system—which was adopted precisely to *ensure* fairness and equal treatment—the dynamics of information and access work to favor those with higher educations.

Although there are not enough data to say for certain at this point, the research tends to suggest as much. For each Golden Rule–type program, getting the word out—about what the programs offer, who is eligible, when and where applications must be filed, what the procedures are for applying, and so on—proved to be an operational task that was more complicated and consequential than leaders had counted upon. All relied heavily on newspapers, supplemented by churches and private schools, both of which had incentives to inform their clienteles that vouchers would be available. In addition, leaders could expect some and perhaps many people to find out through word of mouth, once the information was released through the more formal, organizational channels. The importance of these media varied across cities. In Milwaukee, private schools were the most important sources of information—a reflection, no doubt, of their prior organization and leadership in creating the program—whereas in Indian-apolis and San Antonio, newspapers were most important.

If all low-income people were entitled to a voucher, or if admissions were based on lottery or some other random means, then the flow of information would not be so crucial. Virtually all eligible families would eventually find out, and timing would not matter. But in a world of limited vouchers, with availabilty determined by who gets in line first, early access to information makes a big difference. And these are the ones who read newspapers everyday (in English), who are already connected to private schools and to churches, and who are motivated enough to pay attention and pick up the information they need on their own. Although all sorts of people may fall into these categories, the deck is unintentionally stacked in favor of eligible parents who are the most highly educated.

The Student-Sponsor Partnership does not suffer from this problem. Although the demographic data on SSP are not as detailed as on the other programs — it has not carried out surveys of parents or guardians, for instance, so we have no data on their education levels — the available evidence suggests that there is no skimming involved. This is what we would expect, given that students are handpicked for the program based on need and that motivated parents cannot determine who is selected. Unlike the other programs, all SSP students are minorities. Virtually all, between 80 and 90 percent, come from families without two parents. Less than 10 percent were previously in private schools. On average, they are about two grade levels behind the norm on entering the program. Although researchers need to learn more about SSP, its goal is to seek out and save the truly disadvantaged; and it appears that, by centrally controlling the admissions process, it has succeeded in bringing in the kind of students it wants to help.

This comparison of programs is instructive but it does not mean that Golden Rule–type programs must emulate SSP if they are to reduce skimming. Most obviously, they can alter their program designs in two simple ways. First, they can reject first-come, first-served admissions in favor of more balanced methods, such as picking voucher recipients by random draw after an extended application period. And second, they can take the information dissemination process more seriously, tailor it better to low-education families who are less likely to find out on their own, and adopt more aggressive outreach programs — perhaps working closely, as SSP does, with public school teachers and guidance counselors to identify children who are in special need of new educational opportunities.

REASONS FOR PARTICIPATING

A common criticism from school choice opponents is that parents cannot be counted on to make choices by reference to sound educational criteria or values. Parents — especially low-income parents — supposedly care about practical concerns, such as how close the school is or whether it has a good sports team, and put little emphasis on academic quality and other properties of effective schooling. As a result, they not only fail to make good decisions for their children, but they also fail to give schools strong incentives, in competing for parent support, to provide high-quality education (e.g., Carnegie Foundation for the Advancement of Teaching 1992).

These claims are based on a selective view of what little evidence there is on the subject, most of which comes from studies of public school choice arrangements that give parents little to choose from. How can parents choose on the basis of academic quality if the schools they are allowed to choose among are pretty much the same? Clearly, the best way to observe what motivates parental choice is to look at contexts in which they have choices to make.

Before private vouchers, perhaps the most suggestive data on the bases of parental choice came from the Milwaukee public voucher program. Although the number of private sector choices is limited, parents are still allowed to choose between public and private. Witte's data on Milwaukee reveal that low-income parents in the voucher program cite academic quality as the most important reason for using the voucher, followed by discipline and the general atmosphere of the school—clear indications that their choices are driven by educational concerns (Witte et al. 1993, 1994). Voucher parents are also more frustrated and dissatisfied with the public schools than parents who remain in the public sector. Yet this motivation—which appears to derive from the same concerns for academics, discipline, and atmosphere—receives somewhat less emphasis. (I'll return to the dissatisfaction issue in the next section.)

Private voucher programs ought to provide even better evidence because opting into them gives parents the entire private sector to choose from and thus greater opportunities to act on their own values. As the following chapters indicate, the evidence they yield is strikingly consistent with Witte's findings for the public voucher system. Indeed, the results for the two Milwaukee voucher programs, one public and one private, are virtually identical. More generally, across all three Golden Rule–type programs, parents uniformly indicate that academic quality is their most salient reason for participating. Discipline is typically highly ranked, as is the school's general atmosphere. And frustration with the public schools is a consistent complaint; in each program, more than 80 percent of the parents say that it is either an important or very important reason for choosing vouchers.

One caveat needs to be kept in mind. These programs remain small and do not reflect a cross section of their target population. The parents who participate are better educated and more motivated than low-income parents who do not participate, and the fact that they rank school effectiveness issues highly does not mean that the other parents would do the same. They may not. Additional research is needed to determine what the gap actually is and how the full range of parents approaches the task of school choice.

Still, the evidence presented here helps fill the missing contours of our knowledge. And to the extent it does, it challenges the jaundiced, often patronizing view of parents that prevails in parts of the literature—especially of low-income parents, who, critics say, cannot be trusted to make their own decisions (e.g., Wells 1993b). It is of no small weight that the programs being studied here do not target suburbanites, or even average middle class families, but precisely that stratum of society that critics regard as the least capable or responsible. The evidence suggests that, even within this stratum, parents who use vouchers put substantial emphasis on educational concerns in making their choices about schools.

Student Performance

Parental choice is not an end in itself, of course. The point of a choice system is to put parental choice to use—in shifting children out of bad schools and into better ones, in holding schools accountable for their performance, and in giving schools strong incentives to develop high-quality programs—for the ultimate purpose of providing children with a rewarding educational experience. The bottom line is not whether parents make good choices. It is whether children are better off.

For most Americans who think about such things, from parents to policy makers to researchers, this translates first and foremost into a question of whether children learn more. In the debate over school choice, as a result, evidence on learning is often regarded as the acid test of school choice (e.g., Witte 1992; Haertel et al. 1987).

At present, the question of whether children learn more under a choice system is difficult to evaluate empirically. The changes that parental choice sets in motion take time to be realized. Children have to settle into their new schools and be shaped, slowly and incrementally, by their new settings. Schools, in turn, must come to terms with their new incentives and adjust their ways of doing things. It is a mistake to think that, even in a well-functioning choice system, students will suddenly show huge gains in achievement (although some may). Ideally, a confident evaluation calls for studies of systems that have been in place for many years.

The existing data on student learning are sketchy. Massive attention has been directed to Witte's study of the Milwaukee public voucher plan, which does have measures of student performance and which points to mixed results. But the program itself is only a few years old, and, for the reasons I suggested earlier, this evidence has little to tell us about the effects of school choice. As for systems of public school choice, there is some evidence that student performance has improved in the more established systems. East Harlem is the best-known example

(Fliegel 1994). But most choice-based reforms are too new to generate conclusive evidence on student performance at this point, and there are few studies along these lines.

Eventually, private voucher programs should represent an important source of data on achievement. For now, though, both the programs and the research are too young to be useful. Indianapolis has no achievement data. The preliminary evidence from Milwaukee and San Antonio shows that students in the voucher programs score higher on standardized tests than kids in public schools do. But researchers have yet to control for all the other factors, aside from vouchers and private school attendance, that might account for these differences, and they do not have the necessary data at this point to do what is required. Even if they did, I still wouldn't expect much of a performance boost for voucher students because the programs are so new.

The best data on student performance, oddly enough, come from the Student-Sponsor Partnership, which in most respects is the least studied of the four programs. Fortunately, it is also the oldest program and thus the one that has had the longest time to shape children's lives. Its organizers have not collected data on student learning per se, but they have been diligent in tracking the progress of their students and in collecting data on graduation and college attendance rates. On these grounds, SSP's success is nothing short of spectacular. Although its children are chosen precisely because they are seriously at risk of dropping out, some 70 percent of them actually graduate from high school within the program—compared with 39 percent in New York City public schools and about 29 percent in poverty-area New York schools. And of the kids who graduate, a whopping 90 percent go on to college. It seems clear that vouchers have made an important contribution to these children's lives.

This may tell us something about the value of markets, especially in light of recent sudies suggesting that New York Catholic schools do a better job of keeping students in school and equipping them to learn than public schools do (Hill et al. 1990; the Blue Ribbon Panel on Catholic Schools 1993; University of the State of New York 1993). But it may also tell us something about the power of mentoring and other aspects of SSP's unique design. Either way, vouchers appear to have done wonders within this framework.

SSP aside, the jury is still out when it comes to the issue of student performance, and it will be for some time. We need more experience with choice programs, and we need better studies and better data. Private voucher programs, assuming they continue, will help make this possible.

PARENT SATISFACTION

Learning is certainly a crucial outcome of schooling, but it is not the only aspect that contributes to the well-being of children. Standardized tests, moreover, measure only some aspects of learning and may not always do that especially well. To get a more accurate and broadly based view of how well children are doing, we need to look at a wider range of indicators. We need to recognize that many of the important aspects of schooling are intangible: they are qualities that people recognize or sense when they experience them but that tend to defy formal measurement.

In a choice system, the people whose judgments matter most are parents. They may not be experts, but they know what they want for their children, they know what they are looking for in a school, and they can give you their summary judgments of how well schools—and their kids—are doing on a range of dimensions. This is important evidence. It is subjective, to be sure, but it is anchored in direct experience, it reflects the kinds of intangible judgments that are needed to assess important components of schooling, and it addresses a fundamental issue that needs answering about any school system: whether it pleases the people it is supposed to be serving. This is a performance issue, no less than student learning is.

For now, data on parent satisfaction offer the best evidence available on the impact of vouchers. Witte's reports on the Milwaukee public voucher system have already shown that voucher parents are substantially more satisfied with their new private schools than public school parents are with their public schools. Although the size of the satisfaction gap depends on what aspect of schooling is being evaluated—from learning to discipline to textbooks to opportunities for participation—voucher parents are consistently more satisfied than their public school counterparts, whatever the issue (Witte et al. 1993, 1994).

The data coming in from the private voucher programs reinforce Witte's initial results. The study of Milwaukee's PAVE program purposely surveyed its parents on the same satisfaction items and found that PAVE parents are not only considerably more satisfied than public school parents across all issue areas but even more satisfied than the parents in the public voucher program. This makes sense because they have more to choose from than the public voucher parents do and they have more opportunities to find schools they are happy with. In both San Antonio and Indianapolis, meantime, the evidence indicates that parents' satisfaction increases substantially, and across a variety of dimensions, as they shift from public to private schools as a result of vouchers.

This is crucial information. But there is also a perplexing side to the satisfaction issue, one that researchers need to pay more attention to. Although the vast majority of voucher parents say they were "frustrated" with the public schools, far fewer say they were "dissatisfied" when asked about specific aspects of the public schools. In Indianapolis, the percentage claiming to be dissatisfied is typically between 20 and 35 percent, depending on the issue, with large majorities saying they were satisfied on each. The same is true in San Antonio, although dissatisfaction seems to run a bit higher there, varying between 25 and 50 percent or so; even in that city, a majority of voucher parents typically indicated that they were satisfied.

A similar phenomenon is apparent if we look at public school parents. In Milwaukee, the proportion of public school parents who actually say they are dissatisfied with their schools varies between 7 percent (textbooks) and 25 percent (discipline), depending on the issue; fully 65 percent say they would give their schools a grade of A or B. In San Antonio, a poor Hispanic community not known for the quality of its public schools, 80 percent of the surveyed public school parents gave their schools an A or B.

These figures are intriguing and may have various explanations.[14] But one deserves special mention. Attempts to measure citizen satisfaction with the full panoply of local government services—police, fire, garbage collection, schools— have long suffered from a subtle problem that has largely gone unrecognized, both by education researchers and by students of urban government.[15] One symptom of this problem is that low-income people, who by objective standards are often provided with lower-quality services, may claim to be quite satisfied, whereas higher-income suburbanites, whose services are objectively of much higher quality, may complain and express their dissatisfaction. A plausible reason for this disparity (when it occurs) is that these groups have different expectations based on their very different life experiences. Low-income people have lower expectations than high-income people and may be more disposed to say they are satisfied. This is especially likely to be true, I suspect, among populations of recent immigrants, who are not used to the kinds of services U.S. governments provide, and among subcultures (such as the Hispanic) that emphasize paternalism and deference to authority.

Simply asking parents whether they are satisfied with their schools, then, ignores the expectations problem and, for low-income populations—which is what we are dealing with in the new voucher research—may tend to exaggerate the positive. Data showing that 80 percent of San Antonio parents give their schools high grades, or that only small percentages of public school parents in various cities are dissatisfied, do not mean that the schools are doing a good job or that parents might not be much happier if they could choose different schools. It may say little more than that their low expectations are easy for public schools to meet.

The most reliable evidence we have at this point is from studies that compare the satisfaction levels of similar populations (e.g., low-income private school parents and low-income public school parents) or that measure changes in satisfaction levels as parents move from one type of school to another, as voucher parents do. These data suggest that vouchers do indeed help parents get into schools that they like better.

Conclusion

The private voucher movement is in its early stages, and research on its programs has only just gotten under way. Even at this point, however, these new programs represent a valuable source of information and insight that begins to fill a serious gap in the existing empirical literature.

The current knowledge gap is a by-product of politics. In the public sector, the education establishment's staunch opposition to vouchers has so far defeated all voucher proposals but one, the pilot program in Milwaukee, creating a situation in which there has been virtually nothing on vouchers to study and no way for researchers to gather the kind of evidence they need. By default, Milwaukee has come to be regarded as the critical test of whether vouchers work, even though its program is so restricted that it makes a poor laboratory for exploring what vouchers can or cannot do.

Thanks to the private voucher movement, there are suddenly a great many voucher systems in operation. These systems, moreover, are based on simple program designs, free of the bureaucratic and political constraints that, in the public sector, have inhibited the operation of choice and made the study of its effects exceedingly difficult and confusing. With the advent of private vouchers, researchers have an array of exciting opportunities for exploring how vouchers actually work and for investigating a range of choice-related issues that in more complex settings would tend to be obscured.

The studies in this volume represent a first attempt by researchers to take advantage of these new opportunities. Their findings are preliminary, and, as in any area of social science, they could change as new data are collected. But for now they take us a step or two in the right direction, and they point the way for others to follow.

On the whole, what they have to tell us about vouchers is positive and encouraging. The evidence suggests that there is indeed a genuine demand for vouchers among low-income families, who respond enthusiastically and in large numbers when given the opportunity to participate in these programs, even when they are asked to pay half the costs. Free to choose, they distribute themselves across a wide variety of private schools; these schools, contrary to the prevailing myth about private sector elitism, appear only too happy to take them in. When poor children have vouchers, they have access, and there is good reason to believe that their educational opportunities are expanded considerably.

Experience from private voucher programs also casts doubt on the myth of parental incompetence. The evidence suggests that participating parents make good choices for their children, or at least make a serious effort to do so, for they appear to be guided by precisely the sorts of educational criteria that concerned parents ought to be guided by—academic quality, discipline, and other indicators of effective schooling. To the extent this is so, moreover, they are probably transmitting the right kinds of incentives to participating schools, which are put on notice that they need to do their jobs well if they are to attract parent support.

There is little hard evidence to document whether children are actually better off as a result of vouchers, but the signs are positive. Graduation and college attendance rates from the Student-Sponsor Partnership suggest that it has had dramatic success in using vouchers to transform the lives of at-risk children, and this is important evidence of what vouchers can do (combined, of course, with the right design). More generally, we also have subjective evidence on parental satisfaction, which indicates that, on a variety of different dimensions, voucher parents are highly satisfied with the schools they have chosen, think the shift from public to private has been a beneficial one, and evaluate their schools more highly than public school parents do. These are important measures of how well students and schools are doing and, even were test scores and other objective data available, would still deserve heavy emphasis. For now, they suggest vouchers are working well for the people who use them.

On the negative side of the ledger, one issue stands out: these programs have given rise to skimming effects. The skimming issue is well worth attention, but it needs to be kept in perspective. The overarching fact is that private vouchers strike a forceful blow for social equity. They are premised on the goal of expanding educational opportunities for low-income families, appear to be succeeding, and deserve great credit for that.

The skimming effect at work here is "internal," favoring some low-income families—those who are more highly educated and motivated—over others. It is predictable, given the underlying dynamics of choice, but it is not inevitable and could readily be lessened or even eliminated with the right program design. Skimming occurs because the Golden Rule model is not designed to prevent it. The most likely suspect is its first-come, first-served rule, which allows the best-informed, most highly motivated families to snatch up a limited supply of vouchers. Were program leaders to change their rules for application and acceptance, and put more effort as well into communication and outreach, they would almost surely see a dramatic reduction in internal skimming.

The skimming issue highlights a fundamental point that is little appreciated in the debate over vouchers: *design is the key*. How vouchers and choice work out in practice turns on the framework of rules in which they are embedded.

The Golden Rule and Student-Sponsor Partnership models illustrate just how different the designs and consequences of voucher programs can be. Both have their pluses and minuses. The Golden Rule programs are simple, flexible, relatively easily managed, allow families and schools a maximum of freedom, are easily extended to large constituencies, and give almost full rein to the power of markets. But the absence of controls threatens to produce certain problems:

internal skimming, the possible exclusion of especially needy children, the possible inclusion of bad or mediocre schools, and so on.

The SSP program, in contrast, is tightly controlled by its organizers. Children are handpicked on the basis of need, schools are selected on the basis of quality and fit, and the scope for choice and markets is somewhat limited. The resulting program appears to have done wonders with its participating children. But how many children can ever participate in such a program? On a grand scale, it threatens to require a heavy administrative superstructure in which many of the advantages of choice would be stifled by the practical necessities of beneficent top-down control.

Although a great deal more research needs to be done comparing these and other program designs, it seems reasonable to suggest that the most productive models for large-scale, public sector voucher programs will lie somewhere in between. Vouchers will not automatically produce the nirvana imagined by free market aficionados in the absence of certain controls. But the controls must be of the right type, and they cannot be so onerous that they undermine the power of choice. The debate over vouchers should, at its heart, be a debate over design. How should the rules be set up to ensure that choice and markets best promote important social values? The pivotal issue is not about free markets versus government but about how government, through the design of an appropriate framework of rules, can harness the power of markets to greatest social advantage.

As private voucher programs expand and multiply, researchers will have increasing opportunities to observe how different designs work out in practice and, more generally, to explore the range of issues—from student performance to parental participation to information to equity and access—that need to be jointly assessed and fitted together in any coherent treatment of vouchers. This is an exciting prospect, and for the first time promises to generate an extensive body of empirical research to inform the public debate. As it does, it may well change that debate dramatically, along with the path of U.S. educational reform.

This prospect, of course, has been at the heart of the movement's game plan from the beginning: to generate evidence that can be used as a powerful weapon in the political struggle for choice-based reform. Whether things will work out as its leaders envision is another matter. Most of the evidence has yet to come in. When it does, it may or may not be as convincing as supporters hope (although I suspect it will be quite positive). Even if the empirical case is overwhelming, it may or may not have much of an impact on the rough and tumble world of power politics, which is often unresponsive to even the best of evidence. Time will tell.

In the meantime, we cannot lose sight of the fact that the private voucher movement is a far more important social phenomenon than a focus on evidence and research alone can suggest. It is a movement that opens new educational opportunities to thousands of disadvantaged children. It is a movement that promotes innovation and change by loosening the grip of established interests. It is a movement that adds fire and momentum to the larger movement for school choice. But above all else, in my view, it is a movement that embodies and advances a new politics of education—a politics that stands traditional alliances on their heads and promises to transform the constellation of pressures that shape our nation's educational policies and practices.

The new politics of education has only just begun to emerge, but its roots are deep in the basic structure of modern American society. Low-income families are trapped in our nation's worst schools. They want the same kinds of educational choices and opportunities that more advantaged families have, yet their demands for radical change have gone unrepresented by their usual political allies—Democrats, the educational estabishment, liberal interest groups—who are tightly bound to the existing system and committed to defending it. Accordingly, the poor are driven to look elsewhere for their champions, and they are increasingly finding them among groups traditionally labeled conservative, where there is a genuine willingness to take on the educational powers that be and, social stereotypes notwithstanding, a genuine concern for using markets and choice to promote social equity.

In the new politics of education, the conservatives have become the progressives, pushing for major change, promoting the causes of the disadvantaged, and allying themselves with the poor. The progressives of yesteryear, meantime, have become the conservatives of today, resisting change, defending the status quo against threats from without, and opposing the poor constituents they claim to represent. In its consequences for the American system of education, this is perhaps the most important political transformation of modern times—and the private voucher movement, as both a creature of the new politics and a major force for its expansion, is right at the heart of it.

Notes

1. The following brief overview of the Milwaukee case is drawn from McGroarty 1994; Peterson 1994; Lieberman 1993; Bolick 1992; Mitchell 1992; Beales 1994; and Beales and Wahl 1995, as well as numerous newspaper articles in *Education Week* and elsewhere.

2. The general findings from this Gallup poll are presented in National Catholic Educational Association 1992, although it does not indicate how public opinion on the voucher issue varies by race. I obtained the figures for African Americans and Hispanics from raw data supplied to me by the NCEA.

3. The Milwaukee case is hardly unique in its dysfunctional organizational design. For a broader perspective on why U.S. politics inherently gives rise to ineffective, excessively bureaucratic arrangements, see Moe 1989, 1990.

4. Some of what I have to say about the movement and its leaders is based on my own

involvement in the choice movement generally and the information I have picked up along the way, much of it from conversations with participants and their associates. I have also relied on the National Scholarship Center 1994; Beales 1994; and various publications by CEO America, including the *Voucher Voice*, their newsletter.

5. Not all activists in the private voucher movement are interested in pressing the larger cause of school choice in the political arena; some, including the leaders of a few local programs, are simply concerned with helping needy children and have no broader political agenda. The leaders at the head of the movement, however, are clearly strong choice supporters with an agenda.

6. This summary account of the Indianapolis program is based on the National Scholarship Center 1994; Beales 1994; and Heise et al. 1995.

7. My summary account of the San Antonio program is based on Martinez et al. 1995; Beales 1994; and the National Scholarship Center 1994.

8. This summary account of Milwaukee's PAVE program is based on Beales and Wahl 1995; Beales 1994; and the National Scholarship Center 1994.

9. I have not included the New York private voucher program, the Student-Sponsor Partnership, in table 1 because it is not designed along Golden Rule lines.

10. My summary account of the SSP program is drawn from Hill (1995), Student/Sponsor Partnership (1993), and data directly provided by Peter Flanigan.

11. All these figures are taken from data directly supplied by Peter Flanigan.

12. More precisely, the top three schools in voucher enrollments now attract 640 of the program's 802 students. These figures are from Sue Freeze, consultant, State School Aids Consultation and Audit Section, Wisconsin Department of Public Instruction, who passed them along via telephone to Janet Beales (June 8, 1995).

13. Except where noted, the findings I summarize below are taken from the papers collected in this volume.

14. For example, the response rates for these surveys are fairly low (they are mail surveys), and there may be a bias in the types of parents responding. The San Antonio researchers have discovered that public school parents who do not respond to the survey are less satisfied with their schools than those who do respond. It is possible, then, that the true satisfaction levels are lower than the survey data suggest, perhaps by a good bit.

15. For background on the literature on citizen satisfaction with governmental services, see, for example, Lyons et al. 1992; Fitzgerald and Durand 1980.

References

Beales, Janet R. 1994. *School Voucher Programs in the United States: Implications and Applications for California*. Los Angeles: Reason Foundation.

Beales, Janet R., and Maureen Wahl. 1995. "Private Vouchers in Milwaukee: The PAVE Program." This volume.

Blue Ribbon Panel on Catholic Programs. 1993. *Report to New York State Commissioner of Education Thomas Sobol.* Albany, N.Y.: State Education Department.

Bolick, Clint. 1992. "The Wisconsin Supreme Court's Decision on Education Choice: A First-of-Its-Kind Victory for Children and Families." Heritage Lecture, Heritage Foundation (Washington, D.C.).

Bridge, R. Gary, and Julie Blackman. 1978. *A Study of Alternatives in American Education.* Vol. 4. *Family Choice in Schooling.* Santa Monica, Calif.: Rand Corporation.

Bryk, Anthony S., Valerie Lee, and Peter B. Holland. 1993. *Catholic Schools and the Common Good.* Cambridge: Harvard University Press.

Carnegie Foundation for the Advancement of Teaching. 1992. *School Choice: A Special Report.* Princeton, N.J.: Carnegie Foundation for the Advancement of Teaching.

CEO America. 1994. "Mission Statement, Support Services, History and Background." Bentonville, Ark.: CEO America.

CEO America. 1995a. *Voucher Voice* (Bentonville, Ark.). Spring.

CEO America. 1995b. "Private Voucher Programs, City Status List." Bentonville, Ark.: CEO America.

Chubb, John E., and Terry M. Moe. 1990. *Politics, Markets, and America's Schools.* Washington, D.C.: Brookings Institution.

Clune, William F., and John F. Witte. 1990. *Choice and Control in American Education.* Vol. 2. New York: Falmer Press.

Cobb, Clifford W. 1992. *Responsive Schools, Renewed Communities.* San Francisco: Institute for Contemporary Studies.

Coleman, James S., and Thomas Hoffer. 1987. *Public and Private High Schools.* New York: Basic Books.

Coleman, James S., Thomas Hoffer, and Sally Kilgore. 1982. *High School Achievement.* New York: Basic Books.

Coleman, James S., Kathryn S. Schiller, and Barbara Schneider. 1993. "Parent Choice and Inequality." In Barbara Schneider and James S. Coleman, eds., *Parents and their Children.* Boulder, Colo.: Westview Press.

Cookson, Peter W. 1994. *School Choice.* New Haven: Yale University Press.

Coons, John E., and Stephen D. Sugarman. 1978. *Education by Choice.* Berkeley: University of California Press.

———. 1992. *Scholarships for Children.* Berkeley, Calif.: Institute of Governmental Studies Press.

Crain, Robert L., Amy L. Heebner, and Yiu-Pong Si. 1992. *The Effectiveness of New York City's Career Magnet Schools.* Berkeley, Calif.: National Center for Research in Vocational Education.

Edelman, Murray. 1985. *The Symbolic Uses of Politics.* Urbana: University of Illinois Press.

Fitzgerald, Michael R., and Robert F. Durand. 1980. "Citizen Evaluations and Urban Management: Service Delivery in an Era of Protest." *Public Administration Review* 40: 585–94.

Fliegel, Seymour, with James Macguire. 1994. *Miracle in East Harlem*. New York: Manhattan Institute.

Friedman, Milton. 1955. "The Role of Government in Public Education." In Robert A. Solo, ed., *Economics and the Public Interest*. New Brunswick, N.J.: Rutgers University Press.

——. 1962. *Capitalism and Freedom*. Chicago: University of Chicago Press.

Haertel, Edward H., Thomas James, and Henry M. Levin. 1987. *Comparing Public and Private Schools*. Vol. 2. New York: Falmer Press.

Heise, Michael, Kenneth D. Colburn, and Joseph F. Lamberti. 1995. "Private Vouchers in Indianapolis: The Golden Rule Program." This volume.

Hill, Paul T. 1995. "Private Vouchers in New York City: The Student/Sponsor Partnership Program." This volume.

Hill, Paul T, Gail E. Foster, and Tamar Gendler. 1990. *High Schools with Character*. Santa Monica, Calif.: Rand Corporation.

Kingdon, John W. 1984. *Agendas, Alternatives, and Public Policies*. Boston: Little Brown.

Kozol, Jonathan. 1991. *Savage Inequalities*.

Lee, Valerie E., Robert G. Croninger, and Julia B. Smith. 1994. "Parental Choice of Schools and Social Stratification in Education: The Paradox of Detroit." *Educational Evaluation and Policy Analysis* 16: 434–57.

Levin, Henry M. 1991. "The Economics of Educational Choice." *Economics of Education Review* 10: 137–58.

——. 1989. "Education as a Public and Private Good." In Neal E. Devins, ed., *Public Values, Private Schools*. London: Falmer Press.

Lieberman, Myron. 1993. *Public Education: An Autopsy*. Cambridge: Harvard University Press.

Lyons, W. E., David Lowery, and Ruth Hoogland DeHoog. 1992. *The Politics of Dissatisfaction: Citizens, Services, and Urban Institutions*. Armonk, N.Y.: M. E. Sharpe.

Manski, Charles F. 1992. "Educational Choice (Vouchers) and Social Mobility." *Economics of Education Review*.

Martinez, Valerie, Kenneth Godwin, and Frank R. Kemerer. 1995. "Private Vouchers in San Antonio: The CEO Program." This volume.

McGroarty, Daniel. 1994. "School Choice Slandered." *Public Interest*, no. 117 (fall).

Milwaukee Public Schools. 1993. *1992–93 Report Card: District Report*. Milwaukee, Wisc.: Milwaukee Public Schools.

Mitchell, George A. 1992. "The Milwaukee Parental Choice Program." Milwaukee: Wisconsin Policy Research Institute.

Moe, Terry M. 1989. "The Politics of Bureaucratic Structure." In John E. Chubb and Paul E. Peterson, eds., *Can the Government Govern?* Washington, D.C.: Brookings Institution.

——. 1990. "The Politics of Structural Choice: Toward a Theory of Public Bureaucracy." In Oliver E. Williamson, ed., *Organization Theory: From Chester Barnard to the Present and Beyond*. Oxford, Eng.: Oxford University Press.

———. 1995. "School Choice and the Creaming Problem." In Thomas A. Downes and William A. Testa, eds., *Midwest Approaches to School Reform*. Chicago: Federal Reserve Bank of Chicago.

Nathan, Joe, ed. 1989. *Public Schools by Choice*. Saint Paul, Minn.: Institute for Learning and Teaching.

National Catholic Educational Association. 1992. *The People's Poll on Schools and School Choice: A New Gallup Survey*. Washington, D.C.: National Educational Association.

———. 1985. *The Catholic High School: A National Portrait*. Washington, D.C.: National Educational Association.

National Scholarship Center. 1994. *Just Doing It: First Annual Survey of the Private Voucher Movement in America*. Washington, D.C.: National Scholarship Center.

O'Malley, Charles, and Associates. 1994. *Private Education Issues*. Vol. 3, no. 2. Annapolis, Md.: Charles O'Malley and Associates.

Ornstein, Norman J., and Shirley Elder. 1978. *Interest Groups, Lobbying, and Policymaking*. Washington, D.C.: Congressional Quarterly Press.

Peterson, Paul. 1995. "A Critique of the Witte Evaluation of Milwaukee's School Choice Program." Paper delivered to the Harvard University Center for American Political Studies.

Rasell, Edith, and Richard Rothstein. 1993. *School Choice: Examining the Evidence*. Washington, D.C.: Economic Policy Institute.

Student/Sponsor Partnership. 1993. *Student/Sponsor Partnership Annual Report, 1993*. New York: Student/Sponsor Partnership.

University of the State of New York. 1993. *Roman Catholic Schools in New York State*. Albany: University of the State of New York.

U.S. Department of Education. 1992. "Public Opinion on Choice in Education." Washington, D.C.: Center for Choice in Education.

Walsh, Mark. 1995. "Possible High Court Test of Private School Vouchers." *Education Week* 15, no. 1 (September 6): 18.

Wells, Amy Stuart. 1993a. *A Time to Choose*. New York: Hill and Wang.

———. 1993b. "The Sociology of School Choice." In Edith Rasell and Richard Rothstein, eds., *School Choice: Examining the Evidence*. Washington, D.C.: Economic Policy Institute.

Willms, J. Douglas, and Frank H. Echols. 1993. "The Scottish Experience of Parental School Choice." In Rasell and Rothstein, eds., *School Choice*.

Witte, John F. 1991. *First Year Report: Milwaukee Parental Choice Program*. Madison: University of Wisconsin, La Follette Institute of Public Affairs.

———. 1992. "Private School vs. Public School Achievement: Are There Findings That Should Affect the Educational Choice Debate?" *Economics of Education Review* 2 (December): 371–94.

Witte, John F., Andrea B. Bailey, and Christopher A. Thorn. 1992. *Second Year Report: Milwaukee Parental Choice Program*. Madison: University of Wisconsin, La Follette Institute of Public Affairs.

——. 1993. *Third Year Report: Milwaukee Parental Choice Program.* Madison: University of Wisconsin, La Follette Institute of Public Affairs.

Witte, John F., Christopher Thorn, Kim M. Pritchard, and Michele Claibourn. 1994. *Fourth Year Report: Milwaukee Parental Choice Program* Madison: University of Wisconsin, La Follette Institute of Public Affairs.

Young, Timothy W., and Evans Clinchy. 1992. *Choice in Public Education.* New York: Teachers College Press.

2

Private Vouchers in Milwaukee: The PAVE Program

JANET R. BEALES and
MAUREEN WAHL

Introduction

By most accounts, the Milwaukee public schools are not performing well. Four-year graduation rates have fallen from 79 percent in 1971 to just 44 percent in 1993.[1] Those students that do make it through to the twelfth grade have an average grade-point average (GPA) of 2.18 on a four-point grading scale.[2] For African-American students, who make up 58 percent of the public schools' enrollment, the statistics show even worse levels of academic achievement.[3]

- Just 23 percent of African-American tenth-grade students score at or above the national average on standardized tests in reading and math compared with their white peers—62 percent of whom score at or above average in reading, and 60 percent of whom score at or above average in math.[4]
- The average GPA of African-American high school students is 1.38 compared with 2.10 for whites.[5]
- In the 1992–93 school year alone, one out of five African-American high

The authors wish to thank the following people for their input and suggestions: Sue Freeze, Dennis Kaluzny, Sheryl Kelber, Dan McKinley, Susan Mitchell, Terry Moe, Raymond Ng, and John Witte. We would also like to extend our appreciation to the supporters of Family Service America and the Reason Foundation who made this research possible.

school students dropped out of school. White students fared only slightly better, with roughly one out of eight dropping out.[6]

As performance has grown worse, it has also grown more costly. Between 1973 and 1993, constant inflation-adjusted per pupil spending has increased 21 percent, from $5,820 to $7,030 annually (in 1993 dollars).[7] Not surprisingly, the deterioration of academic quality, even in the face of greater spending, has led to a loss of confidence in public education. A 1992 survey of Milwaukee residents shows that 65 percent of respondents believe that students are less prepared for work today than they were thirty years ago; 53 percent believe students are less prepared for college. Given a choice of public or private schools, just 22 percent of Milwaukee residents said they preferred public schools; 76 percent said they would prefer a private school.[8] Another 1992 survey found that 89 percent of its respondents rated the Milwaukee public schools unfavorably, with 29 percent advocating a "complete overhaul."[9]

Public schoolteachers in Milwaukee seem reluctant to send their own children to the public schools. Half the public schoolteachers in central Milwaukee send their children to private schools, according to a University of Wisconsin study.[10]

Rising dissatisfaction from both within and without the school system has pressured the state and local governments to embark on a number of reforms over the last decade. Significant among these is the Milwaukee Parental Choice Program (MPCP), implemented by the state legislature in 1990–91 through the leadership of Wisconsin State representative Annette "Polly"Williams. The first of its kind in the nation, the MPCP gives low-income students government-funded tuition vouchers to attend any one of roughly a dozen nonreligious private schools in Milwaukee. In 1993–94, about 750 students participated in the MPCP program.

But the private sector has also taken a leadership role in school reform. In 1992, business and religious organizations joined to establish Partners Advancing Values in Education (PAVE), a privately funded school choice program for low-income students. Unlike the MPCP, tuition vouchers from the PAVE program may be used at any private school in Milwaukee, including religious schools. PAVE served roughly 2,370 students enrolled in 102 different private schools during the 1993–94 school year. Compared with similar privately funded voucher programs around the country, PAVE is distinguished by being the largest program and the only one to operate alongside a government supported school choice program.

The latter circumstance affords a unique opportunity to compare the PAVE program with the MPCP and the Milwaukee Public Schools. Doing so will provide information about what kinds of parents and students tend to participate

Table 1   School Choice in Milwaukee at a Glance

	Partners Advancing Values in Education (PAVE)	Milwaukee Parental Choice Program (MPCP)
PROGRAM		
Year begun	1992–93	1990–91
Source of funding	Private foundations, businesses, and individuals	State of Wisconsin
Portion of tuition paid by program	50 percent (up to $1,000 for grades K–8; $1,500 for grades 9–12)	100 percent [a]
STUDENTS		
Number of students participating (1993–94)	2,370	750
Eligibility		
Economic	Low income (below 185 percent of the poverty level)	Low income (below 175 percent of the poverty level)
Grade level	K–12	K–12
Residence	City of Milwaukee [b]	Milwaukee Public School District
SCHOOLS		
Number of schools	102	12
Type of school	Private, including religious	Private, nonsectarian (other restrictions apply)

[a] The MPCP voucher is equal to the amount of state aid per pupil, or $2,984 in 1993–94.
[b] Students residing in the county of Milwaukee are eligible for PAVE scholarships at the secondary level.

in each program, why they made the choices they did, and what kinds of academic gains have been realized by students (see table 1).

Partners Advancing Values in Education (PAVE)

BACKGROUND/HISTORY

The PAVE program grew out of the Milwaukee Archdiocesan Education Foundation, a foundation supporting Catholic schools. This nonprofit foundation provides an array of financial support services to Catholic schools to further educational opportunities for Milwaukee children.[11]

Despite the fact that 66 percent of those enrolled in Milwaukee's inner-city Catholic schools were non-Catholics, the tenuous financial position of both the schools and the families with children enrolled in them was seen as a "Catholic problem," says Daniel McKinley, founder of the foundation and executive director of PAVE.[12] Thus, in 1990 the foundation's board of directors embarked on a strategic planning process designed to "take the program from helping a central core of the city to serving the whole city," says McKinley. To do this, it joined forces with other religious and nonreligious private schools in the city to coordinate a broad-based financial support plan for private education.

It was during the final stages of this planning process that the Golden Rule Insurance Company established the Educational CHOICE Charitable Trust in Indianapolis to provide tuition scholarships to children from low-income families. Using it as a model, the board of the Milwaukee Archdiocesan Education Foundation combined its $800,000 trust with funding from other private sources to create PAVE—a scholarship plan giving children a choice of any private school, not just Catholic or religious schools.

One of the chief contributors to PAVE outside the archdiocese was the Lynde and Harry Bradley Foundation, a Milwaukee-based foundation providing financial support to various education, research, and public policy efforts. The Bradley Foundation pledged $500,000 annually to the PAVE program for three years beginning in 1992. Funding for PAVE has since been augmented by many smaller business and individual donors and a number of major donors. These include the DeRance Foundation ($400,000) and Johnson Controls, Northwestern Mutual Life, the Wisconsin Electric Power Company, and the Siebert Luthern Foundation, each of which contributed $100,000 annually for five years.

PARTICIPATION

In 1993–94, PAVE disbursed more than 2,370 scholarships—up from 2,089 in 1992–93—valued at roughly $1,642,000. The PAVE program grants scholarships, up to a capped amount, for half the amount of tuition at any participating private school selected by the student's parent or guardian. Only children living within the city boundary of Milwaukee who qualify for the federal free or reduced-price school lunch program are eligible to receive PAVE scholarships.

Although originally conceived to serve students in grades K–8, PAVE received numerous requests for scholarships at the high school level. In response, PAVE set up a special fund to assist secondary-school students. Scholarships for elementary and middle school students are capped at $1,000. High school students may request scholarships up to $1,500 and may reside outside the city of Milwaukee.

Ninety-two private elementary schools and ten high schools accepted 2,370 students with PAVE scholarships in 1993–94 (406 were high school students). Paying half the tuition amount up to $1,000 for elementary students and $1,500 for secondary students, PAVE scholarships average $542 and $1,321 respectively.[13]

By comparison, the MPCP program serves roughly 750 students in twelve independent private schools, including two high schools specializing in education for at-risk students. MPCP vouchers are valued at $2,984 and cover full tuition at each participating school.[14]

OPERATIONS

The PAVE program differs somewhat from other privately funded choice programs in how it distributes scholarships. Rather than granting scholarships directly to students on a first-come, first-served basis, PAVE coordinates with a private school administrator at each participating school. One-page scholarship applications are available at the PAVE office, libraries, community centers, and the participating schools. The tuition grant applications ask the student's name, address, and telephone number. It also asks for the name of the school the student plans to attend and the school's tuition. Parents must also mark a box signifying that their child qualifies for the federal free or reduced-price lunch program.

After selecting the private school for which they hope to receive a PAVE scholarship, applicants meet with the school's PAVE administrator. Assuming that space allows, and that the applicant meets school admission standards, if any, the applicant and the school jointly fill out the remainder of the application and send it to PAVE. The signature of both the student's parent or guardian and the school administrator are required. The school is responsible for verifying that the student meets PAVE's financial eligibility requirements.

This arrangement gives discretion to local administrators, who know the circumstances of the families and students they serve. In addition, administering the scholarship program, from the standpoint of PAVE, is made easier, minimizing costs. (PAVE's overhead costs, including the cost of a full-time PAVE administrator, total 7 percent of annual costs and are paid out of a separate fund.)[15] Low-income families tend to be mobile and difficult to keep track of; some own neither cars nor telephones. By working through a local contact in close touch with the applicant family, PAVE can easily locate applicants and award scholarships.

Roughly half the PAVE scholarships are awarded to low-income students who were enrolled in private schools before the advent of PAVE. Recognizing that low-income families often have difficulty paying tuition, PAVE organizers decided to dedicate some of their resources to stabilizing those children already enrolled in private schools.

Payment is made on behalf of each student twice a year and mailed to the school. Parents must cosign the check—a procedure intended to empower parents by directly involving them in the payment process, according to McKinley. Scholarships from PAVE are granted on a yearly basis, with no multiyear commitment. However, the scholarships may be renewed if the student continues to meet PAVE's eligibility requirements and is in good standing with the school.

Scholarships are distributed fairly evenly between new entrants and continuing students, says McKinley. At the direction of PAVE, 45 percent of the scholarships were granted to students already enrolled in the private schools during PAVE's first year of operation. The remainder were granted to students new to private education, with 31 percent of the total going to students transferring from public schools and 24 percent to young children entering grade school for the first time.[16] PAVE's roots in an archdiocesan scholarship fund may account for its commitment to serving a comparatively higher proportion of continuing private education students.

In 1992–93, its first year of operation, PAVE received 4,094 applications, nearly double PAVE's capacity, despite the requirement that parents contribute to tuition. In 1993–94, an additional 2,200 applications were filed with PAVE.

PAVE's application process and eligibility criteria also differ from those of the MPCP. PAVE's eligibility requirements are broader than the MPCP, encompassing greater numbers of low-income children. To determine scholarship eligibility, PAVE uses the federal free and reduced-lunch program, which is calibrated to 85 percent above the poverty level, equivalent to $26,583 in 1993–94 ($27,380 in 1994–95) for a family of four. The MPCP program uses a cutoff of 75 percent above the poverty level, or $25,113 for a family of four in 1993–94 ($25,900 in 1994–95). According to Russ Whitesel, senior staff attorney with the Wisconsin Legislative Council and a consultant in the design of the MPCP, the figure of 75 percent was derived from a number of measures used to assess poverty levels in Milwaukee when the MPCP was established.[17]

The one-page applications for the MPCP are available from the Department of Public Instruction (DPI), the governor's office, and the participating private schools. Whereas the DPI sends press releases to Milwaukee newspapers and radio stations every year announcing the availability of MPCP vouchers, the Milwaukee public schools have done little, if anything, to formally publicize the choice program since it was created in 1990.[18] In 1993–94, by order of the legislature, for the first time information about the MPCP was included in a brochure describing various district programs that is published annually by the Milwaukee public schools.[19]

The MPCP applications must be filed between May 1 and June 30 with the school or schools the student has selected for enrollment in the upcoming September. The applicant must give her or his name, address, and grade level, name of the public school the student was enrolled in during the previous year, and name of the school to which the student is applying. To verify income eligibility, applicants mark the appropriate box in a chart listing household income levels; applicants must also list their social security number and sign the application.

Although the participating private schools may not screen applicants for admission, most schedule an informational interview with the applicant and parent to discuss school policies and parent and student responsibilities. The school must inform the student within sixty days after receiving the application whether or not the student has been accepted (acceptance or rejection is based only on capacity). If more applications are received than there is space available, a lottery is used. Siblings of students already enrolled in the school and continuing MPCP students are exempt from the lottery and given priority enrollment. These administrative policies were developed by an advisory council representing participating private schools.

Like PAVE, the MPCP has been oversubscribed every year of its operation. Between 1990 and 1993, the number of students turned away for lack of available private school capacity has been 236 (1990), 168 (1991), 357 (1992), and 307 (1993) students.[20]

The Wisconsin legislature enacted strict regulations when it created the MPCP, among them that no more than 49 percent of students in any one grade level at each private school may be MPCP students. (The schools are permitted to accept fewer MPCP students than allowed by the cap.) In addition, no more than 1 percent of the total Milwaukee public school population may participate in the MPCP—a limit that has never been exceeded owing to restricted private school capacity. In the 1994–95 school year, these limitations were lifted slightly, to 65 percent and 1.5 percent, respectively.

SCHOOLS PARTICIPATING IN PAVE

The PAVE scholarships may be used at any private school selected by the recipient family. To date, PAVE's reach has been impressive, helping pay the tuition of 2,450 low-income students during 1993–94 in 102 of Milwaukee's 108 private schools.

All but twenty of the private schools participating in PAVE are religiously affiliated, and thus nearly 95 percent of PAVE students attend such schools, with more than half (60 percent) attending the fifty Catholic parochial schools participating in PAVE.[21] However, PAVE appears to be having the greatest positive impact on non-Catholic Christian, Jewish, and Muslim schools, which have proportionately higher numbers of students receiving PAVE scholarships than do the Catholic schools. At least one in four students in the non-Catholic Christian and Jewish schools uses a PAVE scholarship. Almost half the students in Muslim schools participate in PAVE. By contrast, just one in eight Catholic school students receives assistance from PAVE (see table 2).

Table 2   Elementary Schools Participating in the PAVE Scholarship
             Program, 1993–94.

Elementary School Affiliation	1993–94 Total Enrollment	Number of PAVE Scholarships	% of Total Enrollment on PAVE Scholarships	Value of Average Scholarship
Catholic	9,256	1,222	13	$561
Lutheran	2,658	395	15	557
Other Christian	631	187	30	581
Jewish [a]	134	39	29	1,000
Muslim	26	12	46	574
Independent	1,663	178	11	752
TOTAL	14,368	2,033	—	—

[a] Tuition at the Yeshiva Elementary School, the only Jewish school for elementary school students in Milwaukee, averages $3,300 annually.
SOURCE: PAVE

In addition, seven of the twelve independent private schools in the MPCP program enroll students with PAVE scholarships. Because regulations restrict the supply of MPCP vouchers at these schools, some students use PAVE scholarships to attend schools in the MPCP program when MPCP vouchers are available.

PARENT SURVEYS AND METHODOLOGY

Much of the information about the PAVE program comes from surveys of parents whose children received PAVE scholarships. Commissioned by the Lynde and Harry Bradley Foundation, the survey of PAVE families was conducted by Family Service America (FSA), a national nonprofit corporation providing services, education, and advocacy for families in need through its 290 member agencies. The purpose of the survey was to describe the families that were granted PAVE scholarships during the 1992–93 academic year to determine the amount of parental involvement in the participating schools and to evaluate parental satisfaction with the PAVE program. Information about academic performance was collected in FSA's *Second Report of the PAVE Scholarship Program* and is reported below. The data will serve as the foundation for a three-year longitudinal study of the PAVE program.

The FSA survey design was based on a series of surveys, conducted by Professor John F. Witte of the University of Wisconsin at Madison, to assess the attitudes and demographics of families participating in the publicly funded Milwaukee Parental Choice Program.[22] Although the FSA survey does not include all the questions contained in Witte's survey (FSA did not ask about household income, for example), there are many points of comparison. The Witte survey provides two useful control groups: low-income families who participated in the MPCP and low-income families whose children remained in the Milwaukee public schools. Unless noted, all the following statistics come from the FSA survey (including the *First-Year Report of the PAVE Scholarship Program*) and the *Third-Year Report, Milwaukee Parental Choice Program*, by John F. Witte.

DATA COLLECTION

FSA surveys were mailed in May 1993 to every family having at least one PAVE scholarship recipient during the 1992–93 academic year. Three weeks after the initial mailing, surveys were sent to all nonresponding families in an attempt to raise the overall response rate. Of the 1,549 families who were mailed surveys, 955 (62 percent) returned completed surveys; 35 (2 percent) of the surveys were returned to FSA as undeliverable. FSA received surveys representing all eighty-five participating schools. Sixty-four elementary schools had a 50 percent or greater response rate among surveyed families; all high schools had at least a 50 percent response. The responses of individuals have been kept confidential by aggregating the survey results.

SURVEY RESULTS:
DEMOGRAPHIC CHARACTERISTICS OF PAVE FAMILIES

Chief among the questions about school choice is what kinds of families are likely to transfer their children from public to private schools. Limited as it is in size, and shaped by the specific design features discussed above, the PAVE program can only partially answer that question. What we do find is that the survey results about family demographics are consistent with those collected from the privately funded choice program operating in San Antonio, Texas, the only other program to have conducted parent surveys using public school control groups. This suggests that PAVE can tell us a great deal about how similarly structured programs would perform but less about how a full-scale state-supported program would perform.

The PAVE program targets low-income families without regard to race, ethnicity, gender, or religious preference. By accepting only students from low-income households, the program has reached its goal (see table 3).

Race. Roughly half (46 percent) of the female parents or guardians of PAVE students are white. African Americans are the next largest group (37 percent). Hispanics (3 percent), Asians (2 percent), and Native Americans (2 percent) made up the remainder of the respondents (see table 3).

Table 3   Percentage of Milwaukee Students, by Race

	PAVE [a] (%)	MPCP [b] (%)	Low-Income Children Milwaukee Public Schools (%)	Milwaukee Catholic Schools (all elementary students) (%)	All Low-Income, School-Aged Children in the City of Milwaukee (%)
White	46	3.0	29	92	42
African-American	37	78.0	55	3	45
Hispanic	13	17.0	10	3	10
Asians	2	0.2	4	1	—
Native American	2	1.0	1	1	—
Other	—	—	—	—	4

[a] Race of mother or guardian of PAVE student.
[b] Applied to the MPCP 1990 to 1992.
SOURCE: *First-Year Report of the PAVE Scholarship Program, Third-Year Report, Milwaukee Parental Choice Program*, and Bureau of the Census data from the Demographics Services Center, state of Wisconsin. *U.S. Catholic Elementary and Secondary Schools, 1993–94, Annual Statistical Report on Schools. Enrollment and Staffing* (Washington, DC.: National Catholic Education Association, 1994).

Of the four school groups described (PAVE, MPCP, low-income Milwaukee public schools, and Milwaukee Catholic schools), PAVE most closely reflects the racial characteristics of the city of Milwaukee. Fifty-eight percent of all school-age children in Milwaukee are nonwhite, and 54 percent in PAVE are nonwhite. By comparison, 97 percent of MPCP students are nonwhite, 71 percent of low-income public school students are nonwhite, and 8 percent of Catholic school students are nonwhite.

Comparing PAVE students with low-income students in Milwaukee public schools, whites, Hispanics, and Native Americans are overrepresented in PAVE. Because close to half of PAVE participants are drawn from private schools, however, one would expect that PAVE would mirror the current private school population rather than the public school population from which just 31 percent of PAVE students is drawn. In fact, PAVE students fall somewhere between the public school and Catholic school populations—which enroll 65 percent of all privately enrolled elementary school students—with regard to the number of minority students represented.

When the racial composition of elementary students in the Catholic parochial schools of Milwaukee is compared with the PAVE elementary students, the PAVE program includes a higher proportion of minority students (54 percent) than the Catholic schools (less than 8 percent).[23] Because roughly 60 percent of PAVE scholarships at the elementary level are given to students who choose

Table 4   Marital Status of Parents of Milwaukee Students

	PAVE (%)	MPCP (%)	Milwaukee Public Schools (low income) (%)
Married/remarried	43	23	35
Divorced	23	16	13
Single (never married)	22	40	32
Separated	9	12	11
Widowed	3	4	2
Living together	1	5	6

SOURCE: *First-Year Report of the PAVE Scholarship Program,* and *Third-Year Report, Milwaukee Parental Choice Program.*

Catholic schools, and because 54 percent of all PAVE students are racial minorities, PAVE makes it possible for proportionately more minority students to attend Catholic schools—and private schools generally—than otherwise would do so.

Demographic characteristics, particularly with respect to race, also differ significantly between MPCP families and the low-income public school control group. The MPCP has proportionately more African-American students and fewer white students compared with the Milwaukee public school low-income student population as a whole (see table 3). Student participation may be influenced by characteristics of the private schools themselves. The two schools serving the largest numbers of MPCP students, the Harambee School and the Urban Day School, which together enroll approximately four hundred MPCP students, primarily enroll African-American students. Various characteristics of the participating schools may explain why a higher proportion of African-American students choose to participate in the MPCP than their numbers in the public schools would indicate.

Marital Status. Most PAVE families are headed by a single parent. Roughly a quarter of the PAVE parents have never been married; another quarter are divorced. Forty-two percent of PAVE parents are married or remarried. An even greater proportion of families in the low-income public school group and the MPCP are headed by a single parent. Thirty-five percent of low-income public school parents are married; interestingly, the number of married parents in the MPCP program is even lower, 23 percent (see table 4).

Because PAVE scholarships cover only half the cost of tuition, families with two parents may be in a better financial position to participate in such a program. Alternatively, single parents might be more inclined to apply for the MPCP

voucher, which covers total tuition costs. Also, because the PAVE program includes religious schools, parents with strong religious values, which typically
emphasize marriage and family life, may be more inclined to seek out the PAVE
scholarships rather than enroll their children in the MPCP or the public schools,
which exclude religious teachings.

RELIGIOUS PREFERENCE

Results from surveys of PAVE parents regarding religious involvement are
not conclusive. Less than 2 percent of the respondents expressed no religious
preference. The majority (53 percent) identified themselves as Catholic; 41 percent, Protestant, 2 percent, Jewish, and 1 percent, Muslim. Although the survey
of MPCP parents did not collect data about religious affiliation, it did ask parents
to rate the importance of "maintaining religion/belief" compared with the importance of education. Fifty-eight percent thought, as a goal, it was *as* important
as education. Twelve percent responded that religion/belief was more important,
and 30 percent stated that education was of greater importance. The response
rates of the public school parents were similar to those of the MPCP parents,
suggesting that religion/belief did not play a part in the decision to transfer from
the nonsectarian public schools to the MPCP, which also excludes religious
education by excluding religious schools. Unfortunately, the FSA survey did not
attempt to assess the degree of importance religion and belief played in the lives
of PAVE parents. Therefore, we can not determine whether religion played a
significant role in the decision by parents to participate in PAVE. We can only
report their religious affiliation.

AGE OF PARENT

The average age of PAVE parents is thirty-five, with a range of twenty to
seventy-nine. The average number of children in a PAVE family is 2.3 compared
with 2.6 in MPCP families and 3.2 in low-income public school families.

EDUCATIONAL ATTAINMENT OF PARENT

The educational attainment of PAVE parents is similar to that of MPCP
parents. Roughly 30 percent of female parents/guardians from each group
earned, at most, a high school diploma or its equivalent; almost half had continued their education, taking some college courses. Just 7 percent of PAVE female
parents and 6 percent of MPCP female parents were college graduates. Likewise,
just 3 percent of PAVE female parents and 4 percent of MPCP female parents
reported having an eighth-grade education or less (see table 5). Male parents/
guardians had similar responses.

Table 5   Educational Attainment of Female Parent/Guardian

	PAVE (%)	MPCP (%)	Milwaukee Public Schools (low income) (%)
Eighth grade	3	4	12
Some high school	12	12	25
General Equivalency Diploma	5	10	9
High school degree	25	22	25
Some college	46	45	26
College graduate	7	6	3
Some postgraduate	3	2	1

SOURCE: *First-Year Report of the PAVE Scholarship Program*, and *Third-Year Report, Milwaukee Parental Choice Program.*

Educational attainment differences are greatest between Milwaukee public school low-income parents and the two school choice programs. The difference is especially noticeable among the least-educated parents—those with less than a high school degree. Among choice parents, from either PAVE or the MPCP, just 10 percent fell into this category; among low-income public school parents, 37 percent of females had less than a high school education. The differences were also great at the other end of the scale—college-educated parents. Fifty-six and 53 percent of PAVE and MPCP parents, respectively, had attended college; just 29 percent of low-income MPS parents had done so.

(Interestingly, although MPCP parents are more educated than public school parents on average, their incomes are slightly lower than those of low-income public school parents. MPCP households averaged $11,625, whereas average household income for public school low-income families was $12,130 for the years 1990 to 1992 combined. The FSA survey did not collect household income data for the PAVE families.)

These findings suggest that educated parents are more likely to seek educational opportunities for their children and that school choice is perceived as such an opportunity. Opinion surveys of PAVE and MPCP parents show that both groups overwhelmingly rated "educational quality" as "very important" in their decision to participate in school choice. Both groups also tended to report higher levels of parent involvement in their children's educations compared with public school parents.

The survey of PAVE parents did not ask about the educational expectations they had for their children. Educational expectations, however, were high for both MPCP and low-income public school parents. Eighty-seven percent of

MPCP parents expected their child to attend college or graduate school compared with 72 percent of parents of low-income public school students. In general, the more education obtained by parents, the greater their educational expectations for their children. This could explain why more-educated parents opted
for some type of choice program for their child.

   Public versus Private School Parents in PAVE.   Despite coming from different school backgrounds (public or private) PAVE students have similar demographics. If one breaks out the responses of the 400 PAVE parents who indicated
their child had at one time been enrolled in public school, there is little difference between the survey responses of those parents and the 529 low-income
PAVE parents who have had their children enrolled in private schools all along.
This similarity applies not just to race, marital status, age, religion, and education
level but to qualitative measures such as the parents' level of involvement in their
children's schools.

   One possible explanation for the similarities between seemingly different
populations (parents new to private schools and parents who have always elected
for private school) is that PAVE may make possible private education for parents
who would have opted for private schools in the first place and been willing to
pay for them but whose financial resources were insufficient to cover full tuition
costs. PAVE bridges the financial gap for these low-income parents.

SURVEY RESULTS: HOW FAMILIES LEARNED ABOUT PAVE

   The most common source of information about the PAVE program was the
private schools themselves, where 54 percent of parents learned about PAVE.
Because just 45 percent of PAVE students had been enrolled in private schools
before PAVE, some parents—roughly 10 percent—who had children either in
public school or entering school for the first time, may have been investigating
private schools before they learned about PAVE. From a policy standpoint, this
could mean that PAVE provided support to first-time private school parents who
would have chosen private schools even in the absence of a voucher.

   Because parents could check more than one source of information on the
parent survey, however, some double counting may be involved. Additional research is needed to determine what the original source of information was for
PAVE parents.

   Other sources of information marked off on the survey were friends and
family (14 percent), church (11 percent), newspapers (10 percent), and televi-
sion/radio (9 percent). Community centers played a small role in informing
parents about PAVE (less than 1 percent) (see table 6).

   Most MPCP parents, in contrast, heard about the program by word of
mouth, through friends and family. Private schools were a source of information

Table 6   How Parents Learned about the School Choice Program

	PAVE	MPCP (1992)
Friends or relatives	14	44
Television or radio	9	21
Newspapers	10	24
Private schools	54	22
Churches	11	3
Community centers	<1	4

SOURCE: *First-Year Report of the PAVE Scholarship Program*, and *Third-Year Report*, *Milwaukee Parental Choice Program*.

for just 22 percent of MPCP parents, probably because, unlike the PAVE program, MPCP students had to have been enrolled in the public schools before participating in the MPCP. Half the students in the PAVE program were already enrolled in a private school before applying for a scholarship. Both the PAVE and the MPCP programs distribute applications directly to the participating schools.

A revealing difference between the two programs is that PAVE families were far more likely to learn about the program through church than were MPCP families (11 percent of PAVE families compared with only 3 percent of MPCP families). This could indicate, on the one hand, that PAVE parents attend church on a more regular basis and so would be more likely to hear about a school choice program. On the other hand, because PAVE includes religious schools and the MPCP does not, churches would be more likely to know of, and promote, the PAVE program, particularly if a private school were affiliated with that church. Neither the MPCP nor PAVE targeted churches for disseminating applications; however, both specifically targeted private schools, and for PAVE, this included religious schools. Such schools could have been a conduit for information to their affiliated churches about the PAVE program.

SURVEY RESULTS: PARENTAL ATTITUDES AND BEHAVIOR

Foremost among the reasons parents gave for their participation in the PAVE program was educational quality. Eighty-nine percent of parents rated educational quality as "very important," more than any other consideration listed. Educational quality was also important to MPCP parents, 87 percent of whom marked it as "very important."

The other reasons parents gave for participating in school choice were similar for both the PAVE program and the MPCP, with discipline, general atmo-

Table 7   Factors Affecting Decision to Participate in a School Choice
               Program, as Reported by Parents, 1990–92

	Very Important PAVE MPCP (%)		Important PAVE MPCP (%)		Somewhat Important PAVE MPCP (%)		Not Important PAVE MPCP (%)	
Educational quality	89	88	11	11	4	1	<1	0
Discipline	72	77	22	21	4	3	1	0
General atmosphere	73	76	21	21	5	3	1	1
Financial considerations	77	71	18	22	4	5	<1	2
Special programs	48	67	29	26	13	4	11	3
Location	60	62	22	19	12	14	6	5
Frustration with public schools	65	61	18	22	10	11	8	6
Other children in chosen school	36	39	25	29	14	13	25	19

SOURCE: 1993 Surveys of PAVE parents, Family Service America, and *Third-Year Report of the Milwaukee Parental Choice Program*, University of Wisconsin.

sphere, and financial considerations being judged "very important" by roughly three-quarters of choice parents (see table 7). Frustration with the public schools also seems to have played a significant role in parents' selections. Although just a third of PAVE parents transferred their students out of public schools, 65 percent of PAVE parents indicated that "frustration with the public schools" was a very important reason for their choice.

Roughly the same number (64 percent) of MPCP parents indicated that their negative experience with the public schools had been a major reason for transferring into private education. Besides indicating widespread dissatisfaction with public education among PAVE and MPCP parents, these figures also indicate that many PAVE parents originally chose private schools because of their dissatisfaction with public education, before the advent of PAVE. Low-income parents who are willing to pay tuition to send their children to private school, instead of sending their children to public school where no financial sacrifice is required, probably perceive substantial differences in quality between the two settings.

The importance of the reasons parents gave for participating in choice differed between PAVE and MPCP participants in just two areas. MPCP parents seemed to place greater importance on other children (siblings) enrolled in the MPCP program. This may be because MPCP families have more children, 2.6 on average, compared with 2.3 children on average for PAVE families.

The second noticeable difference in survey responses was that MPCP families indicated "special programs" played a significant role in their choice far more often than did PAVE families. Seventy percent of MPCP parents marked "special programs" as "very important" compared with just 48 percent in the PAVE program. Because 90 percent of the schools participating in PAVE have a religious orientation—a characteristic distinguishing them from public schools—parents may have considered religion a "special program." It is difficult to know what "special programs" meant to survey respondents, however, so no conclusions can be drawn about this response.

SURVEY RESULTS: PARENTAL SATISFACTION

Overall, parents participating in the PAVE program seem to be highly satisfied with the schools they selected. (As mentioned above, 65 percent of PAVE parents indicated that frustration with the public schools had been a "very important" reason for their selecting a private school.) On questions about school discipline, school location, instructional programs, textbooks, and the performance of the schools' teachers and principals, more than 90 percent of PAVE parents expressed satisfaction (see table 8). By contrast, satisfaction levels among Milwaukee public school parents were lower on each of the eight factors evaluated. Where satisfaction levels differed the most between PAVE and public school parents was in the areas of discipline and student learning. Among PAVE parents, satisfaction levels did not differ significantly between those parents whose children had previously been enrolled in public school compared with those with children previously enrolled in private school.

PAVE parents gave the private school they had selected high grades. Ninety percent rated the schools with an A or B: 56 percent gave their school an A, and 34 percent gave the school a B. Eight percent gave the school a C. Less than 2 percent gave their schools a D or F. The grades MPCP parents gave their schools were good but somewhat lower. The parents who were least satisfied with the schools their children were enrolled in were those low-income parents with children in the Milwaukee public schools (see table 9).

Parents in the MPCP were also very satisfied with their schools, although not quite as satisfied as the PAVE parents. Almost 90 percent of MPCP parents were satisfied with school discipline, school location, instructional programs, textbooks, and staff performance (see table 8).

Ninety-six percent of PAVE parents were satisfied with the amount their child learned in school; 94 percent were satisfied with opportunities for parental involvement. Again, satisfaction on these two parameters was also high for MPCP parents, although not as high as for PAVE parents. In the MPCP, 88 percent were satisfied with the amount their child learned; 91 percent were satisfied with the opportunities for parental involvement in the private school they had chosen.

Table 8   Parental Satisfaction with the PAVE Program, the MPCP, and the Milwaukee Public Schools (MPS) as Reported by Low-Income Parents in Each Program

	Very Satisfied (%)			Somewhat Satisfied (%)			Somewhat Dissatisfied (%)			Very Dissatisfied (%)		
	PAVE	MPCP	MPS	PAVE	MPCP	MPS	PAVE	MPCP	MPS	PAVE	MPCP	MPS
Textbooks	47	42	29	47	47	63	3	6	6	1	5	1
School location	52	46	41	42	37	44	4	10	10	1	6	5
Opportunities for parent involvement	55	52	36	40	39	54	3	4	8	1	4	3
Teacher's performance	52	54	40	43	35	48	3	6	9	1	5	3
Program of instruction	53	45	33	43	44	56	3	6	9	1	5	5
Principal's performance	50	48	37	43	38	48	4	7	9	2	6	5
Amount child learned	54	52	36	42	36	47	3	6	13	1	6	4
Discipline in the school	51	43	27	42	41	48	4	9	17	2	7	8

SOURCE: *First-Year Report of the PAVE Program*, Family Service America, and *Third-Year Report of the Milwaukee Parental Choice Program*, University of Wisconsin.

Table 9   Grades Given by Parents to Children's School

Grade	PAVE (%)	MPCP (%)	Milwaukee Public Schools (%)
A	56	35	26
B	34	38	39
C	8	19	24
D	1	2	8
F	1	5	3

SOURCE: *First-Year Report of the PAVE Scholarship Program*, and *Third-Year Report, Milwaukee Parental Choice Program*.

Parent participation in both their child's education and school appears to be higher among choice families than public school families. Parents of children in the PAVE program or the MPCP were more likely to read to their children or work on math or writing, for example. Parents' reported involvement was slightly higher for MPCP families than it was for PAVE families. For example, 40 percent of MPCP parents indicated that they helped their children with reading and math at least five times a week. For PAVE parents, 38 percent helped their children with reading and 30 percent helped their children with math five or more times a week. (Figures for PAVE are for elementary-school-aged children only.) Ninety-six percent of PAVE parents and 97 percent of MPCP parents reported attending parent-teacher conferences compared with 84 percent of Milwaukee public school parents.

One might have expected that parents who contributed financially to their children's education (PAVE) would be more inclined to take an active role in helping their children learn. It appears, however, that participation in choice, be it the MPCP or PAVE, is a better predictor of parental involvement than whether the parent must pay for that choice.

Results from the work by John Witte show that, before participation in choice, MPCP parents were more involved in their children's school compared with nonchoosing families. Witte's data indicate that choice may appeal to a more motivated parent. But Witte's data also show that parental involvement increases after parents have switched, suggesting that there is something about either the school chosen or the act of choice itself that is a motivator in its own right.

Academic Performance

PAVE STUDENT PERFORMANCE

Early evidence collected by Family Service America indicates that PAVE students outperform their public school counterparts on standardized tests. This difference holds not just against other low-income public school students but for the public school student population as a whole and for students in the MPCP. In fact, twice as many PAVE students, in percentage terms, score at or above the 50th percentile on the Iowa Tests of Basic Skills (Iowa Basics) than do low-income Milwaukee public school students.

We must be cautious when drawing conclusions about the effects of the PAVE program on academic performance because our data are limited. We don't know, for example, how much of the difference in performance between PAVE students and public school students is attributable to what students learned in the private schools or what they learned before entering the PAVE program. We were not able to control statistically for factors such as income levels or parental education. In addition, any voluntary program automatically introduces a selection bias, which shows up in the type of student who opts into school choice programs. Bias could also be introduced in the survey and test evaluation process. Parents who are satisfied with their children's education, it could be argued, would be more likely to return completed surveys and release test score data to researchers. Because of these limitations in the research and analysis of the PAVE data, we can only present preliminary conclusions. Additional research and analysis are needed to clarify some of these questions.

In its *Second-Year Report of the PAVE Scholarship Program*, Family Service America obtained results from Iowa Basics for 110 of 172 seventh graders enrolled in the PAVE program. (A self-selection bias may have been introduced because test scores were obtained only for those students whose parents agreed to release their child's academic information.) The test results of PAVE students were compared to those of students in the Milwaukee public schools and the MPCP as reported in John Witte's *Third-Year Report of the Milwaukee Parental Choice Program*. (The Witte report aggregates test scores for multiple grade levels, including the seventh grade. Grade-equivalent scores for individual grade levels are not available from the Witte data. Test scores were released to John Witte by the Milwaukee public schools.)

A higher fraction of PAVE students scored at or above the 50th percentile than all other comparison groups (see table 10). In reading, more than 63 percent of PAVE students scored at or above the 50th percentile on the Iowa Basics test compared with just 25 percent of low-income public school students and 17 percent of MPCP students. Similarly, in math, more than 60 percent of PAVE

Table 10   Scores on Iowa Tests of Basic Skills, 1993

	PAVE Students [a] (%)	MPCP Students [b] (%)	Milwaukee Public School Low-Income Students (%)	All Milwaukee Public School Students (%)
READING				
Percent at or above				
50th percentile [c]	63.2	16.7	24.9	29.9
Median (NPR) [d]	58.5	26.0	30.0	32.0
Mean (NCE) [e]	55.5	37.2	38.8	40.9
Standard deviation (NCE) [f]	24.7	15.6	16.9	18.0
	(n=106)	(n=398)	(n=1,212)	(n=1,443)
MATH				
Percent at or above				
50th percentile	60.4	28.3	29.5	35.0
Median (NPR)	57.5	32.0	32.0	36.0
Mean (NCE)	54.1	42.2	39.9	42.7
Standard deviation (NCE)	28.4	17.6	18.9	20.2
	(n=106)	(n=395)	(n=777)	(n=984)

[a] PAVE scores reflect test results of 7th-grade students.
[b] MPCP scores reflect test results of students from multiple grade levels.
[c] Based on National Percentile Ranking (NPR) scores.
[d] Median of NPR scores.
[e] Average of Normal Curve Equivalent (NCE) scores.
[f] Standard deviation of student NCE scores.
SOURCE: *Second-Year Report of the PAVE Scholarship Program*, and *Third-Year Report, Milwaukee Parental Choice Program*.

students scored at or above the 50th percentile as opposed to 30 percent of public school low-income students and roughly 28 percent of MPCP students. Because these scores report only the percentage of students scoring at or above the 50th percentile, not their actual test scores, this measure provides only a general indication of the performance of a student cohort.

Mean and median test scores tell us that PAVE students are, on average, above the national average, but only slightly so (see table 10). Conversely, Milwaukee public school students—from all three control groups—are, on average, significantly below the 50th percentile.

When PAVE students are broken out into two groups—those who had previously attended public school (transfer students) and those who had always attended private school—the differences in achievement are significant. The fifty-two students sampled who had transferred from public schools rated consistently

Table 11   Iowa Tests of Basic Skills: Median Scores for Transfer and
              Private School–Only Students

	PAVE Students transferring from Public to Private Schools (n=52)	PAVE Students Who Have Always Attended Private Schools (n=47)
READING		
Grade-equivalent score [a]	7.2	7.9
National percentile ranking (mean scores)	48.5%	66%
MATH		
Grade-equivalent score [a]	7.1	7.8
National percentile ranking (mean scores)	44%	73%
COMPOSITE		
Grade-equivalent score [a]	7.5	8.2
National percentile ranking (mean scores)	47%	69%

[a] Grade-equivalent scores benchmark test scores to the standard of achievement for each grade level. The first digit corresponds to a particular grade level, while the second digit refers to the number of months beyond that grade level.
SOURCE: *Second-Year Report of the PAVE Scholarship Program*

lower in math, reading, and on the composite score than the forty-seven students who had only attended private schools[24] (see table 11). These results hold not only for NPR scores but also for grade-equivalent scores. (Transfer students include those students who transferred from public schools to private schools before the advent of PAVE. Roughly half the seventh-grade transfer students left the public schools using PAVE scholarships—after attending public schools for six or seven years. The remainder had left the public schools sometime before entering the fifth grade and before the PAVE program was operating.)

Yet, on the basis of available demographic data, the two groups have similar family background characteristics. Both groups come from low-income households. The parents of both groups of students are also similar in terms of race, marital status, age, religious preference, and education level. That is, the demographic characteristics of parents in one group matched those in the other group. Even on qualitative measures, such as level of parental involvement in their children's education, the responses from both sets of parents were essentially the same.

Given that the only significant difference between the transfer group and the private school–only group is their past school environment, the evidence suggests that differences in test scores may be a result of prolonged enrollment in private schools of choice. In other words, private schools may have a positive impact on the academic performance of low-income students.

However, there may be additional variables (such as spirituality or socioeconomic status within the low-income parameters) that may alter these conclusions. Moreover, the small sample size (n=99), drawn from seventh-grade students, makes extrapolation to the K–12 student population problematic. More extensive research is required to verify these preliminary results.

Note that the lower-performing PAVE students in table 11 who had transferred from public schools appear to outperform all other MPS control groups shown in table 10 on academic tests. However, because of the large differences in sample size, more data are needed before meaningful conclusions can be drawn.

MPCP STUDENT PERFORMANCE

Perhaps more puzzling are findings on MPCP achievement levels reported by John Witte in his *Third-Year Report*. On test scores, there is a very significant difference between the PAVE students, who perform well, and the MPCP students, who perform poorly, despite the fact that both groups attend private schools and that some PAVE students attend the same schools as MPCP students.

Research by Witte may provide some answers. In his *Third-Year Report*, he writes:

> The attitudes of parents toward their children's prior public school within MPS may be a reflection of the fact that their children were not doing well in those schools. . . . The absolute level of the [Iowa Tests of Basic Skills] scores indicates the difficulty these students were having prior to entering the [MPCP] program. The median national percentile for choice students ranges from 26 to 31, compared with the national median of 50. The Normal Curve Equivalent, which is standardized to a national mean of 50, ranges from 37.5 to 39.8, which is about two-thirds of a standard deviation below the national average. *In short the choice students in this program enter very near the bottom in terms of academic achievement.*[25] (Italics in the original.)

Therefore, the MPCP appears to receive a higher concentration of low-performing students to start out with compared with the Milwaukee public schools. In addition, the MPCP requires that students attend public school the year before enrolling in the program; therefore these students have not been exposed to private education to the same extent as PAVE students.

The question for researchers is whether these low-achieving MPCP students improve academically once they transfer to schools of choice. Data from Witte's *Third-Year Report* provide some evidence of minor improvements. He reports a slight increase in math scores for MPCP students coupled with a statistically insignificant decline in reading scores.[26]

More research is required to assess fully the impact of both the MPCP and the PAVE program on student achievement. However, as PAVE shows, on average, low-income students in private schools achieve at higher levels than their public school counterparts on standardized tests. These trends corroborate the findings of several other major studies, including research by John Chubb and Terry Moe[27] and James Coleman.[28]

Attrition Rate

Compared with the MPCP, the PAVE program does a better job at retaining students. Of 2,450 PAVE students, ninety-five (or 4 percent) left the PAVE program during the 1992–93 academic year. Over the same time period, fifty students (the difference between the September student count of 620 students and the June count of 570 students) left the MPCP, representing 8 percent attrition.[29] (The attrition rate, which refers to students who leave the school choice program midyear, should not be confused with the dropout rate, which refers to students who leave education altogether.)

To discover the reasons students left the PAVE and MPCP programs, researchers for the MPCP aggregated the reasons of students who left midyear with those who failed to return to the program following the summer break (see table 12). Researchers with the PAVE program present data for only those students who left the PAVE program midyear (see table 13).

With respect to PAVE, if we omit the students whose families became financially ineligible for the scholarships, the attrition rate drops to 3 percent. This is a remarkably low rate for any population but especially so for a low-income population facing greater degrees of financial and other types of instability than the population at large.

Regarding the MPCP, roughly half the students (49 percent) leaving the program enrolled in Milwaukee public schools. Nineteen percent enrolled in Milwaukee contract schools (nonpublic schools), home-school environments, or schools outside Milwaukee. One third (32 percent) enrolled in other private schools, often for religious reasons, according to the *Third-Year Report, Milwaukee Parental Choice Program.*

Because researchers with the MPCP had not expected to analyze the causes of attrition when they designed the study, they had difficulty following up with nonreturning students/families, especially those who had moved out of the area entirely. Results in table 12 reflect this bias and should be viewed as preliminary.

However, several findings are worth noting. Approximately 40 percent of

Table 12   Students Who Left the MPCP and Why

Reason	Number of Students	%
Program quality		
Lack of religious training	8	10.0
Lack of transportation	7	8.8
Income	3	3.8
Application problems	4	5.0
Fee changes	1	1.3
Quality of the choice school		
Poor education	8	10.0
Too disciplinarian	4	5.0
Unhappy with staff	11	13.8
Lack of programs for talented students	1	1.3
Lack of programs for students with special needs	6	7.5
Too segregated	2	2.5
Child expelled	2	2.5
Child/family specific		
Transportation—too far away	6	7.5
Moved	6	7.5
Pregnancy	2	2.5
Quit school	2	2.5
Child custody change	2	2.5
Miscellaneous	3	3.8
TOTAL	78	100.00

SOURCE: *Third-Year Report, Milwaukee Parental Choice Program.*

those MPCP students who left the program indicated they were dissatisfied with some aspect of the school chosen. By contrast, just 6 percent of the PAVE parents whose children left reported dissatisfaction with the school they had selected. Ten percent of the students left the MPCP because of lack of religious training, which is prohibited by state statute in the MPCP schools. By including religious schools, the PAVE program avoids this problem. Also, transportation-related difficulties were cited by almost 16 percent of MPCP respondents yet were absent from the responses by PAVE families. Because the MPCP includes just twelve schools whereas the PAVE program includes 102, families in Milwaukee are more likely to be close to a participating PAVE school than an MPCP school. With a greater supply of schools from which to choose, transportation problems appear to become fewer.

A number of additional factors may help explain why the PAVE attrition rate is half that of the MPCP's. On the one hand, parental satisfaction with the PAVE

Table 13   PAVE Program Students Who Left and Why, 1992–93

Reason	Number of Students	%
Transferred to another school	23	24
Increased family income made student ineligible for PAVE	15	16
Family moved	14	15
Behavioral problems	10	11
Dissatisfaction with school	6	6
Family could not pay other half of tuition	5	5
Expulsion	4	4
Academic performance	2	2
Withdrew to study at home	1	1
No reason	15	16
TOTAL	95	100

SOURCE: *Second-Year Report of the PAVE Scholarship Program.*

program is higher than in the MPCP, and parents have a greater variety of school choices under PAVE. Demographic characteristics may also play a role. Students from two-parent families, which are more common in the PAVE program than in the MPCP, may experience a more stable home environment, which in turn may contribute to more stability in their school environment. Moreover, the average academic performance of PAVE students is significantly higher than that for MPCP students. Students who are succeeding in a particular school may be more inclined to continue their education at that school.

On the other hand, one might expect that the PAVE attrition rate would be higher than the MPCP given the fact that low-income parents may have difficulty maintaining their share of tuition payments from year to year. Yet this does not appear to be the case. Just 5 percent of PAVE families in table 13 indicate that they left the program because of their inability to maintain their share of the tuition payments.

PROJECTING A DROPOUT RATE

If we assume that student behavior, expulsion, academic performance, and "no reason obtained" resulted in the student dropping out of school altogether, then, at worst, the annual hypothetical dropout rate for PAVE elementary and secondary students would be less than 1 percent.

A corresponding figure for K–12 students in the Milwaukee public schools is not available.[30] However, at the high school level, the annual *actual* dropout rate is 17.4 percent.[31]

Conclusion

Although comparisons among the different educational settings are simple to make, drawing accurate conclusions about them is more difficult. The PAVE program and the MPCP program differ in several fundamental ways. The PAVE program requires families of scholarship recipients to come up with half the tuition (some families have obtained additional scholarships or other support to reduce their share of tuition costs); the MPCP parents pay nothing toward private school tuition. A greater diversity of private schools, including religious schools, participate in the PAVE program, whereas the MPCP tightly restricts private school participation. Students receiving MPCP vouchers for the first time must have attended Milwaukee public schools in the previous year. By comparison, roughly half of the PAVE students had already been in private schools before receiving a tuition scholarship.

Because of these and other differences in program design, PAVE and the MPCP may be serving different constituencies within the eligible low-income population. As these two programs demonstrate, school choice programs can be designed in many different ways that may influence what kinds of families are attracted to the program as well as the programs' success in improving student performance.

SUMMARY OF KEY FINDINGS

Parents' answers to survey questions show that PAVE parents tend to be better educated, are more likely to be married, and have higher educational expectations for their children than parents of low-income Milwaukee public school students. It would be inaccurate to say that choice parents are uniformly more advantaged, however. For example, MPCP parents tend to have lower incomes and are less likely to be married compared with low-income public school parents.

Preliminary findings from research on standardized test scores of seventh-grade students show that PAVE students on average outperform both MPCP students and public school students in math and reading. When PAVE students are grouped according to prior school experience (i.e., previously enrolled in private school or public school), the test scores of PAVE students who had attended private school were significantly higher than PAVE students who had attended public school. Yet in all other demographic, family, and other background characteristics surveyed, the two groups were virtually identical. This suggests that the type of school (public or private) is a strong predictor of student academic performance. The test scores also show that lower-performing PAVE students who had been enrolled in public school still outperform the other public school control groups. This indicates that PAVE attracts low-income students who are stronger academically than their public school peers. Additional research is necessary to confirm the preliminary results presented here.

The attrition rate for K-12 students in PAVE is half that of the MPCP, or 4 percent. Reasons for this difference may include the higher parental satisfaction levels reported by PAVE parents, higher levels of academic achievement by PAVE students, and more variety and availability of schools from which to choose under the PAVE program. On the basis of PAVE's attrition rate, it is reasonable to assume that the *dropout* rate of PAVE high school students is also significantly lower than the 17.4 percent annual high school dropout rate of the Milwaukee public schools.

Beyond offering greater academic opportunities to low-income students and broadening access to private education for low-income students, PAVE also benefits the private schools. Roughly one in four students attending non-Catholic Christian, and Jewish schools, and nearly one in two students attending Muslim schools, does so with the financial support of PAVE. For private schools generally, PAVE enables more minority students to partake in private education.

Although the MPCP tends to enroll a higher proportion of African-American students compared with their share of the Milwaukee public school student population, the PAVE program tends to enroll more whites. Because both the MPCP and PAVE are school choice programs and do not award vouchers or scholarships on the basis of race, these differences may stem more from the characteristics of the private schools themselves and less from the appeal of school choice to various racial and ethnic groups. Of all three school populations studied here, PAVE most closely reflects the racial composition of the school-aged population in the city of Milwaukee.

LESSONS FOR WOULD-BE DESIGNERS OF SCHOOL CHOICE

Not only does the design of a school choice program influence what kinds of families will participate, it can also influence its reach. Milwaukee's two school choice programs provide a compelling example of how restrictions on school choice end up limiting the number of students who can participate and the number of school programs that might serve them.

Despite the fact that it involves significant financial costs, the PAVE program is in greater demand among low-income families than the MPCP. In 1993–94, the MPCP received approximately nine hundred seventy applications; PAVE received close to four thousand.

Because legislative constraints have severely restricted choice's reach, just seven hundred forty-six of roughly one thousand MPCP vouchers authorized by the state were used by students to attend private schools. Compared with PAVE, the MPCP limits participating schools to nonsectarian institutions willing to accept the $2,987 voucher amount as payment in full for tuition. Parents who would be willing and able to pay extra for additional school services for their children cannot do so under MPCP rules.[32]

Admission standards at the private schools may not select on the basis of gender, religion, or academic achievement, discouraging or disqualifying some private schools with admissions requirements. No more than 49 percent (65 percent beginning in 1994–95) of the students enrolled at any one private school may use vouchers—a clause that restricts the number of students who can use the voucher while discouraging new private schools from opening that would cater to a primarily voucher-holding clientele.

Moreover, restricting participation to just 1 percent (1.5 percent beginning in 1994–95) of public school enrollment hobbles market dynamics by artificially restricting the market's scale. Only two high schools participate, and both of these are alternative schools for at-risk students. Of 108 private schools in the Milwaukee area, 12 are able and willing to accept students with MPCP vouchers. Consequently, the number of available seats for voucher students are few, and students applying to the choice program have been turned away. In 1993–94, the choice program had 307 more applicants than available seats.[37] In general, regulations, not a failure of choice, have restricted the ability of the MPCP to expand educational opportunities for the low-income population it is intended to serve.

For those students the program does serve, the MPCP is, for the most part, successful. Parents report high levels of satisfaction with the program overall and, in particular, with the amount their children are learning. Test scores from the third year of the program show a significant increase in math scores and a slight decrease in reading scores.[34] Most significant, the number of applications to the MPCP has increased in each of the four years since its inception, and the legislature expanded the program slightly beginning in the 1994–95 school year. The attrition rate, defined as students who leave midyear and students who do not return to the MPCP the following year, continues to hover around 30 percent, however, with half those students returning to the Milwaukee public schools and another third enrolling in other private schools. Increasing the supply of private schools from which parents may choose may help reduce the attrition rate.

A couple of lessons also emerge from the study of the PAVE program. In surveys, PAVE parents most often stated that educational quality was a very important reason for selecting the school (see table 7). And although most parents were pleased with the school they had selected, a number were disappointed. To help families make informed choices about where to send their children to school, information about school and student performance should be made widely available to prospective students and their parents.

Another finding is that the PAVE families who transferred from public schools are nearly identical in demographic characteristics and survey responses to the PAVE families who have had children in private schools all along. Yet, in general, PAVE parents had very different characteristics compared with the control group of low-income public school parents. This suggests that, among low-income families, school choice programs such as PAVE are not reaching the mainstream low-income public school parent but instead are attracting low-income families who would have put their children in private schools in the first place had they been able to afford full tuition. Here again, additional research would be helpful to clarify the motivations of choosing and nonchoosing parents.

SCHOOL CHOICE AS SCHOOL REFORM

Opponents of choice say vouchers will result in a two-tier system. But PAVE scholarships have enabled low-income students to enroll in nearly every private school in Milwaukee, representing, broadly speaking, every type of school. As PAVE has demonstrated, school choice promotes diversity—not just among schools but among students afforded a private school education. PAVE has enabled more low-income and minority students to enter private education compared with their current numbers in the Catholic parochial schools—the only type of school for which we have comprehensive demographic information.

Indeed, it is the current status of public schooling in Milwaukee that has led to a concentration of low-income and minority students in the Milwaukee public schools. Minorities constitute 75 percent of children age five to seventeen enrolled in the Milwaukee public schools but just 58 percent of all children living in the city of Milwaukee.[35] On measures of poverty, 73 percent of Milwaukee public school children come from households with incomes low enough to qualify for the federal free or reduced lunch program, whereas just 55 percent of children living in the city of Milwaukee fall into that category.[36]

"What these numbers tell you is that people who have choice have already exercised it, enrolling their children in private or suburban public schools. Those who are left tend to be poor and black," says Susan Mitchell, a policy consultant who had worked with the Milwaukee public schools.[37] The current system of public education precludes people from seeking alternatives and getting the financial support to do so. Students from low-income families caught in inferior public schools have little recourse.

School choice has the potential to give all children access to quality education. As the PAVE program and the MPCP demonstrate, school choice opens up educational opportunities to low-income and minority students and gives parents the satisfaction of selecting the school that best meets the needs of their own child. In the words of one parent, PAVE "make[s] private education possible for those who could not otherwise afford this privilege. . . . [I] wanted very much for my children to receive the same outstanding education I did so many years ago. Because of the generosity and concern of PAVE donors this wish has become reality."[38]

Notes

1. "Why MPS Doesn't Work: Barriers to Reform in the Milwaukee Public Schools" 7, no. 1 *Wisconsin Policy Research Institute Report* (January 1994): 34.

2. *Grade Analysis Report* (Milwaukee, Wisc.: Office of Educational Research and Program Assessment, Milwaukee Public Schools, 1944); Gary Peterson, research specialist, Milwaukee public schools, 1994. The GPA figure reflects average performance of students enrolled in the twelfth grade, not those who have graduated from the twelfth grade. The average GPA for Milwaukee public school graduates is not available.

3. *1992–93 Report Card: District Report* (Milwaukee, Wisc.: Office of Educational Research and Program Assessment, Milwaukee Public Schools, 1993), p. 8.

4. Interview with Gary Peterson, research specialist, Milwaukee public schools, June 30, 1994.

5. *1992–93 Report Card*, p. 8.

6. Ibid.

7. Correspondence with Sue Freeze, consultant, State School Aids Consultation and Audit Section, Wisconsin Department of Public Instruction, Madison, Wisconsin, July 27, 1994.

8. Gordon S. Black, "The Wisconsin Citizen Survey: A Survey of Wisconsin Public Opinion" 5, no. 1 *Wisconsin Policy Research Institute* (January 1992): 11–12.

9. "Why MPS Doesn't Work," p. 36.

10. "Watch What Teachers Do," editorial, *Wall Street Journal*, August 29, 1994, p. A10.

11. Organizations such as the Milwaukee Archdiocesan Education Foundation, which provide financial support to Catholic schools and tuition support to individuals, exist in many large cities in the United States. The Los Angeles Archdiocese's Education Fund, for example, awarded nearly $4 million in scholarships to 3,600 students attending any one of the city's 290 Catholic private schools in 1993–94. As of November 1993, a capital campaign for the education fund had raised $82 million for endowment and school operation purposes in Los Angeles.

12. Interview with Daniel McKinley, executive director, PAVE, Milwaukee, Wisconsin, November 10, 1993.

13. Dan McKinley, "PAVE Scholarship Report, 1992–94," PAVE, 1434 West State Street, Milwaukee, Wisconsin, March 15, 1994.

14. Interview with Sue Freeze, August 30, 1994.

15. Interview with Dan McKinley, November 16, 1994.

16. Interview with Dan McKinley, April 6, 1994; Maureen Wahl, *First Year Report of the PAVE Scholarship Program* (Milwaukee, Wisc.: Family Service America, 1993): pp. 7–8.

17. Interview with Russ Whitesel, senior staff attorney, Wisconsin Legislative Council, Madison, Wisconsin, July 13, 1994.

18. In his three annual reports evaluating the MPCP, John Witte indicates that infor-

mation about choice has been inadequate: "The most prevalent source of information on choice remains friends and relatives, which basically means word-of-mouth information. That informal communication is more than double the frequency of almost all other sources." (*Third-Year Report Milwaukee Parental Choice Program* [Madison: University of Wisconsin, Department of Political Science and the Robert La Follette Institute of Public Affairs, 1993], p. 4.) Resistance to the MPCP from the DPI and the Milwaukee public schools, which are responsible for the program's implementation, has been strong. In 1992, then Wisconsin State school superintendent Herbert Grover joined with teachers unions to file suit against the MPCP. The Wisconsin Supreme Court ruled that the MPCP did not violate the Wisconsin constitution. ("High Court Upholds Creation of Choice," *Milwaukee Sentinel*, March 4, 1992.)

19. Section 119.23(10), effective 1993–94, of the Wisconsin State Statutes reads as follows: "The department of administration, in cooperation with the board, shall establish a public information campaign to inform the parents of all pupils who are eligible to attend a private school under this section, and the eligible pupils, about the program under this section."

20. Witte et al., *Third-Year Report*, p. 4.

21. Correspondence with Dennis Kaluzny, PAVE, Milwaukee, Wisconsin, July 21, 1994.

22. Witte et al., *Third-Year Report*. Data from the *Third-Year Report* combined survey data from the years 1990 to 1992.

23. Because "white" is combined with "other" in the reporting process of the National Catholic Education Association, which compiles such information, we don't have an exact figure for white students.

24. Maureen Wahl, *Second-Year Report of the PAVE Scholarship Program*, draft (Milwaukee, Wisc.: Family Service America, 1994) pp. 28–29.

25. Witte et al., *Third-Year Report*, p. 8.

26. Ibid.

27. John Chubb and Terry Moe, *Politics, Markets, and America's Schools*, (Washington, D.C.: Brookings Institution, 1990).

28. James Coleman, Thomas Hoffer, and Sally Kilgore, *High School Achievement: Public, Catholic and Private Schools Compared* (New York: Basic Books, 1982).

29. Wahl, *Second-Year Report of the PAVE Scholarship Program*, p. 32; Witte et al., *Third-Year Report*, p. 33.

30. Interview with Gary Peterson, research specialist, Milwaukee Public Schools, September 28, 1944.

31. "1992–93 Report Card: District Report," Office of Educational Research and Program Assessment, Milwaukee Public Schools, p. 8.

32. In July 1995, Wisconsin governor Tommy Thompson signed a bill expanding the MPCP. The plan lifts the cap on the MPCP, allowing up to fifteen thousand Milwaukee children to participate in choice, increases the amount of the voucher to $3,500, and expands the choice program to include private religious schools. On August 25, the Wisconsin Supreme Court halted the expansion with a temporary injunction.

33. Witte, *Third-Year Report*, p. 4.

34. Ibid., p. v.

35. U.S. Bureau of the Census, *Census of Population and Housing, 1990: Summary Tape File 4A Wisconsin* (Madison, Wisc. Department of Administration, July 1994), and *1992–93 Report Card: District Report*, Office of Educational Research and Program Assessment, Milwaukee Public Schools, p. 8.

36. U.S. Bureau of the Census, *Summary Population and Housing Characteristics, Wisconsin*, 1991, and *1992–93 Report Card: District Report*, Office of Educational Research and Program Assessment, Milwaukee Public Schools, p. 8.

37. Interview with Susan Mitchell, the Mitchell Company, Milwaukee, Wisconsin, May 25, 1994.

38. Correspondence from Theresa J. Sawinski, mother of two children who receive PAVE scholarships to attend Saint Alexander Grade School, to PAVE administrators, August 31, 1994.

3

Private Vouchers in San Antonio: The CEO Program

VALERIE MARTINEZ, KENNETH GODWIN, and FRANK R. KEMERER

The moving force behind the San Antonio private school scholarship program is James R. Leininger, a physician and chief executive officer of Kinetic Concepts, a large medical supply company headquartered there. Leininger noted in the mid-1980s that increasing numbers of applicants for employment in his company were functionally illiterate despite having high school diplomas. For a time he tried working within the public school system to encourage reform. Disillusioned, he began looking for other strategies.

An added inducement to Leininger's desire for education reform was frustration with the schooling of one of his four children. Dissatisfied with the public and private choices available, Leininger opted for home schooling. After many frustrating efforts to get his son to focus on learning, the father discovered the behavioral reinforcement value of M&Ms—if his son answered correctly, he got an M&M. If not, dad got the M&M. Experience teaching his son deepened Leininger's interest in education.

When Leininger read in the *Wall Street Journal* about the Golden Rule Insurance Company's privately funded choice program in Indianapolis, he decided to start a similar program in San Antonio. "I have a choice for my kids, but many families don't. I wanted to do something for them," he maintains. Leininger sees the program as a way to prod the Texas legislature to enact a choice program encompassing both public and private schools. In his view, the resulting competition among schools for students is the only way to improve the educational system.

In addition to his company's own substantial financial contribution, Leininger involved the chief executive officers of the USAA Federal Savings Bank and the *San Antonio Express-News* in setting up a $1.5 million tuition scholarship fund to enable low-income San Antonio families to attend private or out-of-district public schools over a three-year period. Concerned about what its publisher termed "the postliterate age," the San Antonio newspaper provided the necessary publicity to launch the program and gave it editorial support.

Under the auspices of the Texas Public Policy Foundation (TPPF), a conservative think tank that Leininger heads, the Children's Educational Opportunity (CEO) Foundation printed its first application form in the *San Antonio Express-News* on April 15, 1992. Latino businessman and civic leader Robert Aguirre was selected as managing director of the foundation. At the press conference announcing the program, Aguirre said that the acronym CEO was intentional "because this is an effort of three local CEOs who have come together and established this foundation." Later, Leininger, Aguirre, and others began aggressively promoting the CEO scholarship program as a model for other cities across the country.

Although the immediate goal of CEO was to provide low-income parents private school choice, TPPF and the funders of CEO also wished to create a groundswell of interest in school choice. In an interview with the authors, Dr. Leininger indicated that a major purpose of his involvement and donations was to use the expected success of CEO to demonstrate the effectiveness of vouchers to members of Congress and to state legislators. He expected that as more CEO-like projects received funding, pressure on legislatures would lead states to adopt voucher programs. The CEO did have an impact on the Texas legislature. In its 1995 legislative session, the Texas Senate passed a pilot voucher program for low-income families that was similar to the CEO program. The Texas House and the House-Senate Conference Committee, however, rejected the measure.

The CEO program received a great boost when, in June 1992, President George Bush invited CEO organizers and the first tuition scholarship recipient, seven-year-old Diana Pavon, to the White House to witness his announcement of a proposal to provide $1,000 tuition scholarships for low- and middle-income families in public or private schools. The Bush measure, termed the "GI bill for children," was later rejected by Congress. With the added publicity generated by the White House ceremony, more than twenty-two hundred applications for the CEO program had been received by September 1992.

The CEO program provides partial tuition scholarships to families so that they may enroll their children in the school of their choice in grades 1–8.[1] Only students who reside in the San Antonio metropolitan area and qualify for free or reduced-fee lunches under federal financial guidelines are eligible. The scholarships cover half a school's tuition, with a maximum of $750. Although low by private school standards in many parts of the country, the CEO scholarship has true value in San Antonio, where the average elementary school tuition is less than $1,500. The average CEO scholarship award is $575.

In the 1992–93 school year, the CEO Foundation provided 936 students with scholarships. CEO chose to give half the scholarships to families whose children were in public schools and half to eligible families whose children were already enrolled in private schools. The rationale for giving the scholarships to students who were not in the public schools was to avoid penalizing those low-income parents who had already sacrificed to send their child to a private school. This decision followed the model of the Educational Choice Charitable Trust in Indianapolis described in Chapter 4 of this volume. CEO selected both sets of recipients on a first-come, first-served basis.

Recipients of the scholarship could use it in the school of their choice. Of the total enrollees, approximately 60 percent enrolled in Catholic schools, 30 percent in Baptist and other Protestant schools, 9 percent in other denominational schools, and 1 percent in nonsectarian schools. The low percentage of nonsectarian schools reflects two factors. First, the overwhelming percentage of private schools in low-income areas of San Antonio are parochial, especially Catholic. Second, many of the churches associated with parochial schools alerted parents to the CEO program so that they were among the first parents to complete applications.

The scholarship program was and remains heavily oversubscribed. Two years after the program began, the waiting list contained more than eighteen hundred students. This number underestimates the number of families who want to participate in the program, for many parents, when told that there was a long waiting list, decided not to apply.

The first CEO voucher recipient's grandfather told President Bush at the White House ceremony that the stipend came as a blessing. Students coming from public schools often speak of escaping an environment they consider unsafe. "My friend got stabbed with a knife during fourth period, so I am thankful I have a CEO scholarship and can go to my new school," said one eleven-year-old student. As noted below, our research about family satisfaction with the program found many parents echoing this sentiment.

School Choice Issues

Many of the purported benefits and harms of choice programs depend on who would actually use vouchers. John Coons and Steven Sugarman (1992) contend that providing educational vouchers to low-income parents would empower them by giving them the same freedom that upper-middle class and wealthy parents enjoy: the ability to send their children to schools teaching the values that parents want their children to have. The proponents of choice expect that, if parents have options, they will become knowledgeable consumers. This will increase the parents' involvement in their children's educations and their satisfaction with schools, which, in turn, will lead to greater learning by students. Supporters of choice expect that, over time, the information and decision-making disadvantages that low-income and less-well-educated parents experience will decline and that most parents will become informed concerning schooling for their children.

Critics respond that publicly funded private programs will favor families with higher incomes who can afford to spend more money on their children's education. The validity of this claim depends in large measure on the design of a choice program: How does the program determine eligibility? What is the size of the voucher? How does the program recruit students? What types of school participate in the program?

Critics also point out that parents with more education are better equipped to make decisions concerning their children's education and that parents who care more about education will participate in choice programs at much higher rates than parents who do not value education highly (Levin 1990). This self-selection process will take from attendance-zone schools many of the most talented students and those who, because of their parents' involvement, may value education highly. Critics hypothesize that the entire choice process will concentrate the better students, both by talent and family values, into one set of schools and will harm the learning environment for children in those schools where the students' parents did not or could not exercise choice.

Studies of *public* choice programs in California, Iowa, and Minnesota indicate that programs increase racial, ethnic, and economic segregation (Rubenstein, Hamar, and Adelman 1992; Willms 1983; Willms and Echols 1992; Carnegie 1992). Magnet schools exacerbate the problem within a school district by selecting students who may have to meet specific academic and test score standards in predominantly minority school districts (Moore and Davenport 1989; Schmidt 1994). In sharp contrast to the skimming effects of most magnet schools, a publicly funded choice program that did not result in students with better grades, test scores, and discipline records leaving their neighborhood schools is the Milwaukee voucher program. This program, which provides full funding for low-income students to attend nonsectarian private schools (Witte and Rigdon 1992), indicates that choice programs, whether public or private, need not skim the best students from attendance-zone schools. In the absence of concerted efforts to reach children from less-advantaged and more at-risk populations, however, choice programs are likely to have a skimming effect.

Opponents of vouchers argue that white and upper-income parents will place their children in schools that require tuition above the base voucher to keep their children away from the perceived dangers and lower educational quality that might occur if their children attended schools with high concentrations of minority or poor children or both. This criticism ignores two points. First, school district lines and existing residential patterns currently segregate students by both ethnicity and income. Second, whether a voucher program increases or decreases segregation will depend on the program's design. On the one hand, if voucher programs are not designed to encourage class and ethnic integration, then they probably will lead to greater segregation. On the other hand, voucher programs may provide a reasonable and politically feasible way of overcoming the segregation that currently exists in the public schools. An important question that voucher supporters must face, however, is whether a program designed so that it would promote integration across either ethnic or economic lines is politically feasible.

A major controversy surrounding private school choice is how large a voucher must be to allow low-income families to exercise private school choice. Coons and Sugarman (1992) contend that vouchers must cover the entire cost of the private school. In contrast, supporters of President Bush's school voucher proposal expected that $1,000 would be sufficient to allow low-income families to exercise effective choice. Despite its obvious importance, until now no empirical research existed that could answer the question.

If private school choice is to be available to low-income families, we must know the amount families can and will invest in their children's education. The 1992 Nobel Prize in economics went to Gary Becker for his pioneering work studying how families invest their resources (Becker 1981). Becker's research has particular importance in education. His theories argue forcefully that the amount of time and money parents invest in each child strongly influences educational achievement. Becker's analysis of educational choice implies that parents may choose educational institutions not only for reasons of educational achievement but also for what Becker refers to as "merit goods." The most prominent among these goods are religious and ethical values and ethnic traditions. Thus, Becker's work suggests that parents may be willing to pay for their children to attend private schools, even if they do not expect that the academic quality will be better than their child's current school. Parents do this because their children will then learn the values that the parents support. Becker's empirical argument brings us back to the normative argument of Coons and Sugarman that school choice is a free speech issue—parents should be free to choose the values they wish taught to their children.

The Research Study

Scholars know comparatively little about the characteristics of families who exercise choice in comparison with those who do not, what motivates them to choose, the characteristics of the school they choose, or the impact of choice on students and families. While a few existing studies examine the effects of school choice among Anglos and African Americans, there is a dearth of information concerning the consequences of choice for Latinos, the category of students in the United States most at risk in education. According to the American Council on Education (Kennedy 1993), Latinos have the lowest high school graduation and college enrollment rates of all races and ethnic groups. Latino students face a complex web of barriers to receiving education: poverty, language, cultural incongruencies, and institutional racism. Moreover, parental involvement in education is lower for Latino parents, and less emphasis is placed on education within the Latino family value structure (Fuller et al. forthcoming; Thomas Rivera Center 1993).

One strategy for breaking the cycle of educational dysfunctions for Latino students is to send them to private schools. Earlier research suggests that Latinos who attend private schools have higher academic achievement and graduation rates and lower dropout rates than comparable Latino students who attend public schools (Murnane 1985; Murnane et al. 1985).

When researchers at the University of North Texas contacted CEO program administrators to learn of their interest in a comprehensive external evaluation, the response was favorable. In fact, CEO officials welcomed an impartial assessment of the scholarship program. To obtain a sample of nonchoosing families with comparable socioeconomic and ethnic characteristics who attended the public schools that the CEO families had left, the researchers contacted the San Antonio Independent School District (SAISD). The SAISD has an enrollment of 60,156 students: 81 percent are Latino, 12 percent are African American, and 7 percent are Anglo. Approximately 80 percent of the district's students receive free or reduced-price meals. Most of the district lies within the incorporated city limits of San Antonio. The superintendent, Victor Rodriguez, proposed to his board that the district participate, provided that the researchers include the district's multilingual choice program in the study. The school board approved the SAISD's participation on this basis.

The SAISD initiated its districtwide multilingual choice program in the early 1980s to enhance the district's foreign-language offerings. The multilingual program is a continuous seven-year program of foreign-language instruction beginning in the sixth grade. Students, who apply in the fifth grade, are admitted on the basis of superior academic performance as evidenced in test scores, grades, and teacher recommendations. The multilingual program includes instruction in the same essential elements required in all Texas public school districts as well as language enrichment through honors classes, accelerated pacing, and individualized instruction. For the 1992–93 school year, the SAISD admitted 675 students to the multilingual program; almost 300 students who met the academic requirements and applied to the program were not admitted because of space limitations. The district does not have a formal waiting list because officials do not want to foster unrealistic expectations among parents. Oversubscription to the CEO and SAISD thematic schools indicates that the demand for school choice within the San Antonio metropolitan area exceeds the supply.

The inclusion of the SAISD multilingual choice program significantly enhances the comprehensiveness and significance of the San Antonio evaluation by providing a comparison group of choosing families within the public school system. It must be noted, however, that the selective admission of the SAISD choice program differentiates it from the CEO program; although some of the private schools participating in CEO are selective, most are not.

The involvement of the SAISD also provides a large sample of nonchoosing families attending neighborhood schools. Thus the research encompasses three primary groups: (1) families choosing private schools, (2) families choosing public multilingual schools, and (3) families in attendance-zone schools.

San Antonio is an ideal site for investigating the consequences of school choice, especially for low-income minority families. More than 85 percent of schoolchildren in the greater San Antonio area are from minority ethnic groups (Partnership for Hope 1991). In 1991, an estimated 18 percent of low-income families residing in the San Antonio Independent School District chose to send their children to private schools, and an additional 2 percent participated in the district's multilingual choice program. In addition, the fact that Texas, unlike many states, does not impose regulatory requirements on private schools allows these institutions to function relatively autonomously. Thus parents truly have a choice among alternative forms of education.[2]

Among the questions the San Antonio project can help to answer are the following: Will a choice program that provides only a partial scholarship take the best students from attendance-zone schools? Will minorities participate in choice programs to a significant degree? To what extent is the teaching of religious values and ethnic traditions a critical component of the decision to participate in a choice program? Will low-income families participate in a private school voucher program if the voucher does not cover the full tuition of the school? What impact does choice have on student achievement? Will parents become more involved and satisfied as they participate in choice programs?

Four characteristics of the San Antonio CEO scholarship program reduce our ability to generalize from its results. First, the program was advertised only in English-language newspapers, probably reducing participation by families in which English is not the primary language. Second, churches provided the other most important source of information about the program, perhaps biasing participation in favor of more-religious families. Third, because the scholarships are limited to students from low-income families, we cannot generalize our results to voucher programs that do not recruit specifically low-income groups. Fourth, because the low-income population of San Antonio is heavily Latino, we are constrained in generalizing about other low-income racial and ethnic groups.

These limitations demonstrate the importance of eligibility requirements and student recruitment on who actually exercises choice. Despite these limitations, however, the two choice programs in San Antonio provide a unique opportunity to study the consequences of school choice. Future research from the San Antonio evaluation will compare the changes in test scores of choice program participants with those of students in attendance-zone schools, examine the reasons that students drop out of both the public and private choice programs, and track parental satisfaction with and participation in both public and private schools over a three-year perid.

Who Chooses?

DATA AND MEASURES

In August–September 1992, we sent mail questionnaires to four groups of choosing families whose children (1) applied and enrolled in the public multilingual program, (2) applied to the public multilingual program but could not enroll due to limited enrollment space, (3) received CEO scholarships and enrolled in private schools, and (4) were already in private schools, applied to the CEO program, and were placed on the waiting list. We included both those who applied and enrolled in the programs and those who were placed on the waiting lists because the families on the waiting list are also "choosers." We made available both English and Spanish versions of the questionnaires. A second mailing to nonrespondents resulted in an average response rate of 48.5 percent (see table 1).

Although the response rates reported in table 1 may seem low, they are higher than any other (published) mail survey to comparable groups (surveys of low-income and minority respondents have notoriously low response rates). Nevertheless, concerned that our sample might be biased, we checked this possibility in the second year's survey. In that year we increased response rates by offering monetary incentives to individuals who applied but did not get into the choice programs. The monetary incentive increased the response rates for those individuals from less than 33.3 percent to 67.1 percent.

Analyses of surveys from individuals who responded to the second wave and received an incentive compared with respondents who did not receive an incentive showed four statistically significant differences: Incentives increased (1) the proportion of Latinos who responded; (2) the response rate of employed females; (3) the response rate of those who were less satisfied with school discipline; and (4) the response rates of parents who were less involved with their child's education. There were no differences between respondents and nonrespondents in

Table 1   Sample Size, Response Rate, and Percentage of
            Total Respondents for Family Groups

Family Groups	Sample Size	Completed Surveys	Response Rate (%)	Total Respondents (%)
CHOOSERS				
CEO participants	900	608	68	22
CEO waiting list	822	270	33	10
Multilingual participants	675	336	50	12
Multilingual waiting list	307	97	32	3
Total for choosers	2,704	1,311	48	49
NONCHOOSERS	3,470	1,375	40	51
TOTAL NUMBER OF FAMILIES	6,174	2,686	44	100

terms of levels of education and income. (We note those instances when a possible response bias might affect the inferences drawn from the first-year survey results.)

In addition to the above groups of choosers, during January and February 1993 we surveyed by phone a stratified random sample of nonchoosing families, that is, families residing within the SAISD whose children attend neighborhood schools. Using bilingual interviewers, we obtained a total response rate of 44 percent.[3] The combined data set of the five groups contains 2,686 cases or families (Martinez, Kemerer, and Godwin 1993). The SAISD nonchoosing families constitute 51 percent; the other 49 percent are choosing families (see table 1).

The survey instruments asked for standard socioeconomic and demographic information as well as opinions regarding children's past educational experiences, extent of parental involvement with children's education, and the importance of education relative to other values and goals. The questionnaires to choice families requested additional information about how families learned of the program and what factors they considered when making the decision to participate.[4] Using the survey results, we analyzed how choosing families differ from nonchoosing families and how families who choose private schools differ from those whose children remain in attendance-zone schools. We expected that three sets of variables relate to being a choosing family: (1) basic socioeconomic and demographic characteristics; (2) characteristics of the family that might create stress on the household, such as divorce and unemployment; and (3) characteristics related directly to education.

Table 2   Annual Family Income by Choosers/Nonchoosers

	CHOOSERS		
	Public	*Private*	NONCHOOSERS
Family Income [a]	*(%)*	*(%)*	*(%)*
0–$4,999	15	11	21
$5,000–$9,999	10	12	18
$10,000–$19,999	32	44	34
$20,000–$34,999	27	34	20
$35,000+	15	1	7
TOTAL NUMBER OF FAMILIES	404	860	1,081

[a] Question: "What is your family/household income range for one year?"

FINDINGS

The CEO private school choice program targets low-income families, and survey results indicate that 27 percent earned less than $10,000, while the largest percentage made between $10,000 and $20,000 (see table 2). CEO respondents, however, are slightly better off than families whose children are in attendance-zone schools, 21 percent of whom reported making less than $5,000 in 1991. The income of multilingual school families is greater than both nonchoosers and CEO participants, which reflects that the program is not targeted to low-income families and attracts a disproportionate number of higher-socioeconomic-status families. The San Antonio data demonstrate that a public choice program that recruits on the basis of academic achievement and does not intensively recruit low-income students will take the higher-income children from attendance-zone schools. In San Antonio, this effect is more pronounced for the public school choice program than for the private voucher program.

A comparison of CEO participants and nonchoosing families indicates that a voucher program such as that proposed by President Bush, which covers only a portion of school costs, will not attract the lowest end of the low-income population. Were the CEO program to increase the percentage of the tuition covered by the scholarship, it is probable that the lowest-income group would be better represented in the program.

Robert Aguirre, one of the founders of the CEO program and an individual instrumental in the spread of CEO programs around the country, has indicated that this research has made the CEO founders aware of the problem. Consequently, they are encouraging CEO-like programs starting up around the country to look for ways to facilitate greater participation by the lowest-income groups. The San Antonio CEO officials did not want to use money that could go to scholarships to pay for advertising and gratefully accepted the free space that the

San Antonio Express-News provided. This limitation to English-language media, however, may have discouraged participation by Latino families in which the parents were not fluent in English. The CEO Foundation now counsels new programs to increase information to non-English-speaking parents and other groups who might be bypassed by traditional media outlets.

Despite the limited size of the voucher and the limitations of information dissemination, the response to the CEO programs shows that substantial demand exists for partial scholarships and that low-income families are willing to sacrifice to send their children to private schools.

The differences observed in the incomes of the CEO, multilingual, and attendance-zone families reflect the unemployment levels in the families and the likelihood that a family will be on one or more types of public assistance. Nearly half of nonchoosing families have at least one unemployed person in the household compared with one-third of private choice families and a quarter of multilingual school families. More than twice as many nonchoosing families receive public assistance (35 percent) as do either public or private choosing families (15 percent).

The disparities between choosing and nonchoosing parent education levels are more striking than differences in income. Choosing parents are considerably more likely to have completed some college than nonchoosing parents (see table 3). In this case, however, the families who choose public multilingual schools are more similar to nonchoosers than the families who choose private schools. More than half of mothers in private choosing families have attended college compared with 37 percent of mothers of multilingual school choosers and only 19 percent of mothers whose children are in attendance-zone schools. Again, had the CEO program been designed and marketed differently, the disparities in education levels of CEO parents may have been reduced.

There are no significant differences in the marital status of San Antonio choosers and nonchoosers. The number of children in choosing and nonchoosing families is, however, quite different. Among attendance-zone families, nearly half had four or more children, compared with fewer than one-third of multilingual school and private school choosers. Fourteen percent of attendance-zone families had more than five children; only 4 percent of private school choosing families have more than five children. More than 40 percent of choosing families have either one or two children compared with only 29 percent of nonchoosing families. These data suggest that if a publicly funded voucher program does not pay the full cost of a child's tuition and no adjustment is made for family size, then the program will discriminate against large families.

One demographic factor that is related to the probability of being a private school chooser is ethnicity. Twelve percent of private school choosers are Anglo compared with only 4 percent of attendance-zone families and 6 percent of multilingual school families (see table 4). Conversely, only 4 percent of private school

Table 3   Educational Level of Parents by Choosers/Nonchoosers

	CHOOSERS		
Education Level [a]	*Public* *(%)*	*Private* *(%)*	NONCHOOSERS *(%)*
WOMEN			
Less than ninth grade	14	4	28
Some high school	9	7	26
High school graduate	39	34	28
Some college	31	48	16
College graduate	6	7	3
TOTAL NUMBER	404	875	1,335
MEN			
Less than ninth grade	14	7	28
Some high school	12	9	22
High school graduate	33	31	30
Some college	32	42	15
College graduate	10	12	4
TOTAL NUMBER	291	678	1,043

[a] Question: "What is the highest level of education you have completed?"

choosers are African American compared with 15 percent of multilingual school choosers and 13 percent of attendance-zone families. There is no bias toward males in either the multilingual or the CEO program. In fact, females are more likely to be chosen for the multilingual school program, probably because females are more likely to be in the top 20 percent of their class and thereby qualify for the program.

On the basis of our measures, a family's educational expectations for its children most clearly differentiate choosing from nonchoosing families (see table 5). The educational expectations of parents who exercised a choice option under the CEO and SAISD programs far exceed the expectations of parents who do not. More than half of choosing parents expect their children to attain graduate and professional degrees, compared with 17 percent of the attendance-zone respondents. More significantly, nearly one-third of the nonchoosing parents expect their children only to graduate from high school. These findings strongly suggest that if parents have high educational expectations for their children, then even low-income parents will expend scarce resources on their children's education.

Along with educational expectations for their children, the biggest difference between nonchoosing and choosing families is in the children's scores on standardized tests. The average normal curve equivalent (NCE) scores of students

Table 4   Race/Ethnicity by Choosers/Nonchoosers

| | CHOOSERS | | |
| | Public (multilingual) (%) | Private (CEO) (%) | NONCHOOSERS (%) |
Race/Ethnicity [a]			
Hispanic	77	84	82
African American	15	4	13
Anglo	6	12	4
Native American	0	1	0
Asian	<1	<1	1
Other	2	<1	<1
TOTAL NUMBER	403	681	1,347

[a] Question: "What is your child's racial identity?"

Table 5   Educational Expectation for Child By Choosers/Nonchoosers

			NONCHOOSERS
	CHOOSERS		San Antonio Independent School District (%)
	Public (multilingual) (%)	Private (CEO) (%)	
Educational Level [a]			
Some high school	<1	<1	3
Graduated high school	4	3	29
Vocational school	<1	2	3
College	43	44	49
Graduate/professional school	52	52	17
TOTAL NUMBER	419	992	1,335

[a] Question: "How far do you expect your child to go in school?"

from nonchoosing families are 27 in math and 27 in reading. The average scores of multilingual students (math NCE = 56, reading NCE = 57) are substantially higher than those of CEO students (math NCE = 47, reading NCE = 46).[5] This difference is not unexpected given the academic performance criterion of the public program.

In sum, the above findings indicate that families involved in the San Antonio choice programs differ significantly from nonchoosing families. Choosing families are less poor, better educated, and smaller than nonchoosing families. Choosing families have significantly higher educational expectations for their children,

Table 6   Grades Given to Schools by Nonchoosers and CEO Parents
            Who Moved Their Children from Public to Private Schools

	NONCHOOSERS (SAN ANTONIO INDEPENDENT SCHOOL DISTRICT)		CEO FAMILIES [b]	
Grade for School [a]	*1991–92* (%)	*1992–93* (%)	*1991–92* (%)	*1992–93* (%)
A	46	44	16	46
B	35	36	29	41
C	13	15	34	12
D	3	3	12	—
F	2	2	8	2
TOTAL NUMBER	1,343	494	347	318

[a] Question: "What overall grade would you give to your child's school last year?"
[b] Includes only CEO families whose child was in a public school in the 1991–92 academic year and in a private school in the 1992–93 academic year.

which encourages them to look for alternatives to attendance-zone schools. Children from choosing families also score higher on standardized tests.

Once again we remind the reader that the design of choice programs strongly affects who participates. If the CEO voucher were larger for families with the lowest incomes, and if it were marketed to a Spanish-speaking audience, then the lowest-income families might participate at higher rates and Latinos might participate at the same levels as Anglos. If the SAISD multilingual choice program did not have performance-based admissions criteria, and if it could accommodate all who applied, then children from low-income families and those with lower test scores would have participated at a higher level.

REASONS FOR CHOICE

Evaluations of nonchooser and CEO parents who used the CEO scholarship to move their child from the public schools reveal substantial differences in their satisfaction levels with public schools. More than half of CEO parents gave their child's previous public school a grade of C or lower (see table 6). By contrast, less than one-fifth of nonchoosers gave their child's school a grade of C or lower. One year later, the satisfaction levels of nonchoosing families remained the same. Parents who moved their child from public schools to private schools, however, were pleased with their children's new schools. Only 13 percent of these parents gave the new schools a grade of C or lower.

Investigation of the reasons for CEO families wishing to move their children

Table 7   Parents' Rating of Children's Learning and with
               Discipline in the Schools

	AMOUNT CHILD LEARNED [b]		SCHOOL DISCIPLINE [b]	
Parents' Rating [a]	1991–92 (%)	1992–93 (%)	1991–92 (%)	1992–93 (%)
Very satisfied	19	60	12	56
Satisfied	40	31	40	33
Dissatisfied	24	5	27	8
Very dissatisfied	18	4	21	2
TOTAL NUMBER	351	326	344	327

[a] Question: "How satisfied were you with the following in last year's school?"
[b] Includes only CEO families whose child was in a public school in the 1991–92 academic year and in a private school in the 1992–93 academic year.

from public to private schools indicated that the key areas of dissatisfaction with public schools were the amount their children learned and school discipline. More than 40 percent of the CEO families whose children previously attended a public school were dissatisfied with the amount their child learned in the public school, and nearly 50 percent were dissatisfied with the discipline in the public schools (see table 7). The levels of dissatisfaction dropped dramatically once the parents moved their children into the private schools. Only 10 percent of these parents were dissatisfied with the amount their child learned or with discipline in the new school.

PUBLIC AND PRIVATE CHOOSERS COMPARED

Although there are tremendous differences in the educational expectations that choosing and nonchoosing parents have for their children, choice and attendance-zone parents are almost exactly alike in terms of the importance they place on education compared with other goals such as having enough money, a good job, and a good place to live (see table 8). Only in the areas of maintaining religious and ethnic traditions do we find significant differences. When comparing the importance of education with the importance of maintaining religious practices and ethnic traditions, private school families are more likely to stress goals other than education, demonstrating that educational goals are not the only rationale for choosing private schools. An important component of the decision to choose a private school is the oppportunity to select a school that will further the family's values. This indicates that the free-speech argument for school choice has validity, at least among low-income families in San Antonio.

When we asked choosing families to indicate the most important reasons for

Table 8   Importance of Education Compared with Other Goals
            among Chooser/Nonchooser Families

Goals [a]	Education more important (%)	Education as important (%)	Education less important (%)	Number
PRIVATE CHOOSERS (CEO)				
Having enough money	69	31	<1	880
Good place to live	53	46	1	876
Having a good job	43	57	<1	872
Maintaining religious practices	16	71	12	872
Maintaining ethnic traditions	33	64	<1	865
NONCHOOSERS (SAISD)				
Having enough money	84	14	2	1,362
Good place to live	66	32	3	1,361
Having a good job	59	37	4	1,356
Maintaining religious practices	49	45	7	1,344
Maintaining ethnic traditions	54	42	4	1,349

[a] Question: "How would you rate the importance of education in your family compared with the following goals?"

selecting alternatives to attendance-zone schools, the leading reason for both multilingual and private school choosers was educational quality (see table 9). (These findings conflict significantly with a conclusion reached by the Carnegie Foundation from its review of the choice literature [Carnegie 1992].) Among the multilingual school choosers, the second most important reason was the availability of special programs. This is to be expected because the emphasis of the multilingual program is on the intensive study of foreign languages. Discipline, the general atmosphere of the chosen school, and religious training were tied as the second most important reason in the decision of private choice parents. Not surprisingly, frustration with public schools was much greater among private school choosers than among multilingual choosers.

PREDICTING WHO WILL CHOOSE A PRIVATE SCHOOL

The preceding discussion indicates that a number of factors, such as size of family, income, and parental educational expectations, correlate with a family's decision to choose a public or private school. We cannot, however, answer questions such as "Which variables are the most important in choosing a private school" and "Are differences in participation rates by Anglos and Latinos caused by the differences in the two groups' education and income levels?" For example,

Table 9   Factors Affecting Decisions to Participate by Public/Private Choosers

Factor [a]	PUBLIC CHOOSERS (MULTILINGUAL)				PRIVATE CHOOSERS (CEO)			
	Very important (%)	Important (%)	Some Importance (%)	Not Important (%)	Very important (%)	Important (%)	Some Importance (%)	Not Important (%)
Educational quality	76	20	4	<1	90	10	<1	<1
Discipline	59	29	8	3	81	16	2	<1
General atmosphere	56	31	10	3	79	19	2	<1
Financial considerations	33	28	18	22	73	22	5	<1
Frustration with public schools	18	22	21	40	63	23	9	6
Special programs	70	24	5	1	52	31	10	6
Religious training [b]	NA	NA	NA	NA	81	15	4	1
Other children in chosen school	22	22	21	36	39	26	14	21
Location	33	24	26	18	50	30	13	7
TOTAL NUMBER	396				956			

[a] Question: "Please rate the importance of the following issues in your decision to participate in the Multilingual/CEO Program?"
[b] This question was asked only of the CEO participants.

Table 10   Public Estimates of the Effect of Selected Variables
            on the Probability of Choosing Private Schools

Variable	Probit Coefficients [a] (T-ratios in parentheses)
Female student	.16***
	(2.27)
Mother's education	.20*
	(6.60)
Educational expectation for child	.30*
	(6.85)
Anglo	.77*
	(3.72)
Religious attendance	.37*
	(11.43)
Dissatisfaction with previous public school	.15*
	(8.96)
Parental activity at school	.22*
	(5.34)
Family on federal assistance	−.32***
	(−2.42)
Number	1,559
Cases of choosing families	262
Correctly predicted	90%
Pseudo R^2	.50%

[a] Includes only those CEO families who moved from public to private schools plus nonchoosing families.
* p < .001,   ** p < .01,   *** p < .05 (one-tailed test).

mothers in choosing families tend to have higher levels of education (see table 3), and a higher percentage of choosers are white than nonchoosers (see table 4). Is the underrepresentation of Latinos a result of lower education levels of Latina mothers? Multivariate analyses allow us to examine this and similar questions.

To answer those questions for the CEO program, we compared those students who moved from public to private schools using a CEO scholarship with the members of our random sample from attendance-zone schools. Using probit regression,[6] we initially placed in the predictive equation all the variables that past research had indicated might affect choice and for which we found statistically significant bivariate differences. (See the appendix for a list of variables and their measures.) In the best-fitting model, eight variables are statistically significant at the .05 level or below (see table 10). Four variables—mother's education, parents' educational expectations for their child, religiosity, and dissatisfaction with the public schools—explain 44 percent of the variation in school choice.

When we add the child's sex, parental activity, whether the family is on federal assistance, and whether the child is Anglo, the explained variation increases to 50 percent. Overall, the probit model correctly predicted 90 percent of the cases.

EXPLAINING CHOICE

Although probit analysis can tell us which variables best predict who chooses, it does not tell us how these variables relate to each other and to the process of choosing a private school. To better understand this process we used path analysis (see figure 1). To understand how different variables relate to choice, move from left to right in the diagram (variables are defined in the appendix). The higher the absolute value of the number beside the arrow between two variables, the stronger is the relationship. For example, the arrow from Latino to mother's education has the number $-.29$. The negative sign on the number indicates that the mothers of Latino children have a lower education than that of other ethnic groups. The .29 indicates a moderately strong relationship. This arrow helps us understand that one reason Latinos have a lower probability of participating in the CEO program is the lower level of the mother's education.

The path diagram demonstrates just how important the mother's education is in the choice process. Mother's education has a low-to-moderate direct impact on private school choice (.20), but it indirectly affects choice through almost every variable in the choice process. Mothers with higher educations are more likely to be dissatisfied with the public schools, and this dissatisfaction has the strongest direct impact on participation in the CEO program. Mother's education also decreases the probability that a family will be in a federal assistance program,[8] a variable that has a small direct impact on private school choice. Mother's education has a strong impact on the parents' educational expectations for their child, the second most important predictor of private school choice. Finally, mother's education leads to greater parental activity in the child's school, a factor that increases the probability that a child will participate in the CEO program.

It is relevant to note that even in the Milwaukee publicly funded voucher program—a program that recruited at-risk, low-income students and paid the entire tuition of the private schools—mother's education was a critical determinant of who participated in the program. This suggests that regardless of race, income, program design, and recruitment strategies, educated mothers are more likely to search out alternatives to attendance-zone schools. Vouchers and scholarships empower parents whose education leads them to want alternatives to their current public school but whose income does not allow either private schools or residence in wealthy neighborhoods and school districts.

Figure 1   Path Diagram of the Decision to Choose a Private School

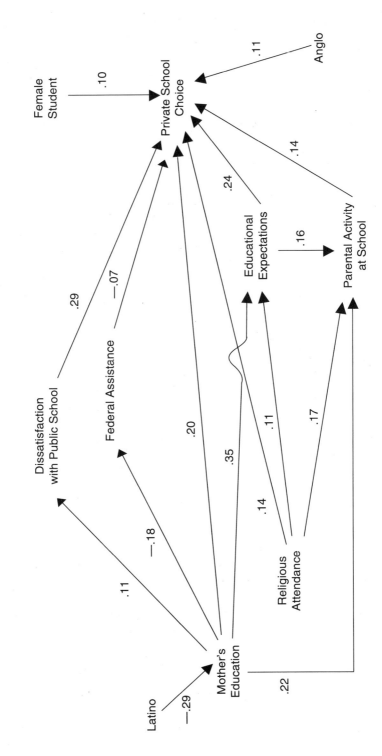

Religious attendance, our measure of the importance of religion to a family, directly affects participation and indirectly increases participation through its impact on educational expectations and parental activity in the school. Educatonal expectations have a strong direct influence on CEO participation and indirectly encourage participation through their impact on parental activity in the child's school.

Two additional variables—being Anglo and being female—slightly increase the probability that a child will participate in the CEO program. Together, however, these variables account for 2 percent of the variation in explaining who chooses.

What emerges from the path diagram is a clearer picture of who chooses and why. Even among the low-income population studied here, more-educated parents have higher expectations for their children, are more active in their child's school, and are more dissatisfied with the education their child receives in the public schools. These factors lead parents to look for alternatives to the public neighborhood school, and the CEO scholarship provided many of the parents with the means to choose the alternative they desired. More-religious parents want to place their child in a school that teaches the values that are important to the parents, which leads them to look for alternatives to public schools. In addition, parents who attend church frequently, regardless of their educational attainment, have high expectations for their child's education and participate in their child's school. As figure 1 shows, these expectations and behaviors encourage private school choice.

Clearly the CEO program has opened up new educational opportunities for many low-income families who otherwise would have no alternative to their assigned public school. The fact that frustration with public school quality and discipline plays a major role in the family decision to choose demonstrates the continuing problems of urban public education. Parents also want schools that include merit goods such as religious training and materials that relate to cultural values and ethnic traditions.

Our results also indicate that although low-income families take advantage of a voucher that pays a portion of private school tuition, even the low tuition involved in the CEO program discourages participation by the lowest-income groups. As noted earlier, the characteristics of choosing families are in part attributable to the design of the CEO and the SAISD choice programs. To have greater participation by the lowest-income groups, a private school scholarship or voucher program must cover a larger portion of the costs and make adjustments to scholarships that account for both income and the number of children in a family.

For a public school choice program to have greater participation by the lowest-income groups, much greater efforts must be made to include these families. It is also likely that any program that uses standardized tests or other performance criteria to decide admission will have lower participation by students whose parents have relatively low levels of formal education.

Conclusion

The CEO Foundation scholarship program has expanded educational opportunities for low-income families in San Antonio. In the process, it has furnished the opportunity to study the effects of private school choice as compared with a public school choice program and attendance-zone schooling. And it has provided its founders with an ongoing, unregulated voucher program to advance the cause of school choice in Texas and beyond.

What is the future of the Children's Educational Opportunity program? Originally, the program was to last three years, which is how long Leininger thought it would take to motivate the Texas legislature to recast the state's educational system. But the slow pace of reform has made CEO officials decide to support current CEO students beyond the initial three years and to add students as funding allows.

Although the San Antonio CEO program has been effectively capped, its founders are aggressively promoting the concept in other parts of Texas and the nation. As part of a CEO national campaign, Robert Aguirre developed a comprehensive planning and operations manual entitled *Educational Choice with Bite! A Privately Funded Model*, which has been widely distributed.[9] In addition to the how-to manual, an eight-minute videotape on the CEO program has been prepared and widely distributed. Leininger, Aguirre, and others at the Texas Public Policy Foundation frequently speak to groups interested in starting a similar program in their communities. The CEO vision is to create new models, new constituencies, and a new climate of opinion leading to public policy changes so that by the end of the century all children in all cities will have the benefits of school choice.

The research in this chapter shows that low-income families in San Antonio who were motivated by unhappiness with the public schooling system, and, in many cases, by the desire for religious-based education, enthusiastically received the CEO voucher program. Although the program design inhibited the poorest families from participating, the CEO program demonstrates that low-income families are as concerned about and supportive of their children's education as middle- and higher-income families. Despite its limitations, the CEO program demonstrates how the vision of one frustrated parent has led to the empowerment of several hundred low-income families in San Antonio and the expansion of private scholarship programs for low-income families throughout the country.

Appendix   Definitions of Variables

Variable	Operationalization
Gender of child	Dummy = 0 if male, 1 if female
Female (male) education	1 = <9th grade, 2 = some high school, 3 = high school graduate, 4 = some college, 5 = college graduate
Female (male) employment	Dummy = 0 if not employed full time, 1 if employed full time
Family income	1 = $0–$4,999, 2 = $5,000–$9,999, 3 = $10,000–$19,999, 4 = $20,000–$34,999, 5 = $35,000+
Receiving assistance	Dummy = 0 if not receiving Aid to Families with Dependent Children (AFDC) or Medicaid, 1 if receiving AFDC or Medicaid
Number of children	Continuous variable, 1–98
Two-parent family	Dummy = 0 if not married, 1 if married
Siblings	Dummy = 0 if 3 or more siblings, 1 if fewer than 3 siblings
Education expectation for child	1 = some high school, 2 = high school graduate, 3 = vocational school, 4 = attend college, 5 = graduate or professional school
Latino	Dummy = 0 if non-Latino, 1 if Latino
Anglo	Dummy = 0 if non-Anglo, 1 if Anglo
Chooser	Dummy = 0 if nonchoosing family, 1 if choosing family
Child's 1992 standardized test scores	Normal curve equivalent (NCE) for reading + NCE for math (range = 2–198)
Material goods versus education index	Importance of enough money + importance of good place to live + importance of good job. Reliability of scale: alpha = .67.
Help at home index	Frequency/week of help with homework + help with reading + help with math + help with writing. Reliability of scale: alpha = .83.
School satisfaction index	How satisfied with school discipline (1 = very dissatisfied, 2 = dissatisfied, 3 = satisfied, 4 = very satisfied)
Contact index	Frequency/year of visit child's classroom + work as volunteer + participate in fund-raising + help in classroom. Reliability of scale: alpha = .72.
School activity index	Frequency/year of join PTA + attend PTA meetings + participate in PTA activities + join other educational organizations. Reliability of scale: alpha = .85.

Notes

1. No student was admitted to a public school in the fall of 1992 when the program was implemented. A few students applied as out-of-district students to attend public schools, but the schools already had waiting lists.

2. Chapter 32 of the Texas Education Code, entitled "The Texas Proprietary School Act," spells out in some detail the criteria necessary for a private school to be accredited by the state. However, a section of that law specifies that state accreditation is voluntary. Furthermore, those schools that want state accreditation are not reviewed directly by the Texas Education Agency (TEA) but by member groups of an umbrella organization of private school organizations called TEPSAC—the Texas Private School Accreditation Commission. TEA defers to its judgment.

3. Mail questionnaires were sent in both English and Spanish to families that did not have phones.

4. The survey instruments were adapted from those used by John Witte to evaluate the Milwaukee choice program.

5. The CEO figures include both students who moved from public to private schools and students previously in private schools. There were no statistically significant differences between public-to-private CEO students and those who were already enrolled in private schools. In fact, the students who were previously in public schools had slightly higher test scores than students previously in private schools. After one year in private schools, a preliminary analysis indicates that the average NCE scores of public-to-private CEO students increased approximately 1 percent. This is a small but statistically significant improvement. Note, however, we were unable to ascertain whether the improvement was attributable to the act of choosing or attending a private school. This is because there were no comparable students who chose a private school but were unable to enroll.

6. Probit regression is a technique designed to measure dependent variables with a limited number of values. In this case the dependent variable—moving from a public school to a private school using a CEO scholarship—has two values. If the child made this move, then his score is one. If the child remained in the public school, then his score is zero.

7. Although path analysis is based on ordinary least squares regression and, for that reason, the final paths to being a chooser are slightly biased, we believe that the paths shown are reliable. The t-ratios and the Dhrymes pseudo R^2 in the probit analysis are almost exactly the same as those in the path analysis.

8. The variable Participation in Federal Assistance Programs probably acts as a surrogate measure of family income adjusted for the number of children. We can get similar results to those shown in figure 1 by dropping Participation in Federal Assistance Programs and adding income and number of children to the equation.

9. The handbook is available from the Texas Public Policy Foundation, 8122 Datapoint Drive, Suite 910, San Antonio, Texas 78229.

References

Aguirre, Robert. 1994. Interview by authors, February 1.

Andrews, John. 1994. Interview by authors, February 1.

Becker, G. 1981. *A treatise on the family*. Cambridge, Mass.: Harvard University Press.

Carnegie Foundation. 1992. *School choice: A special report*. Princeton, N.J.: Carnegie Foundation for the Advancement of Teaching.

Chall, J., and C. Snow. 1982. *Families and literacy: The contribution of out-of-school experiences to children's acquisition of literacy*, Report No. CS 007 254. Cambridge, Mass.: Harvard University Graduate School of Education.

Children's Educational Opportunty Foundation. 1992. *A private scholarship program*.

Coleman, J. S., and T. Hoffer. 1987. *Public and private high schools*. New York: Basic Books.

Coleman, J. S., T. Hoffer, and S. Kilgore. 1982. *High school achievement: Public, Catholic, and private schools compared*. New York: Basic Books.

Coleman, J. S., et al. 1966. *Equality of educational opportunity*. Washington, D.C.: U.S. Government Printing Office.

Coons, J. E. and S. D. Sugarman. 1992. *Scholarships for children*. Berkeley, Calif.: Institute of Governmental Studies.

Fuller, B., S. D. Holloway, C. Eggers-Pierola, X. Liang, and M. Rambaud. Forthcoming. Rich culture, poor markets: Why do Latino parents choose to forgo preschooling? In B. Fuller, R. Elmore, and G. Orfield, eds., *School choice: The cultural logic of families, the political rationality of institutions*. New York: Teachers College Press.

Kennedy, Kristine. 1993. Latinos still trail in college enrollment. *Daily Bulletin*, November 5.

Klingele, W. E., and B. K. Warrick. 1990. Influence of cost and demographic factors on reading achievement. *Journal of Educational Research* 83:276–82.

Leininger, James R. 1994. Interview with the authors, February 1.

Levin, H. M. 1990. The theory of choice applied to education. In W. H. Clune and J. F. Witte, eds. *Choice and control in American education*. Vol. 2. New York: Falmer.

Martinez, V., F. Kemerer, and K. Godwin. 1993. *Who chooses and why? Baseline demographic report, San Antonio school choice project*. Denton: University of North Texas, Center for the Study of Education Reform.

Moore, D., and S. Davenport. 1990. School choice: The new school sorting machine. In W. Boyd and H. Walberg, eds., *Choice in education: Potential and problems*. Berkeley, Calif.: McCuthan.

Murnane, R. J. 1985. A review essay—comparisons of public and private schools: Lessons from the uproar. *Education Studies Review Annual* 10:213–28.

Murnane, R. J., S. Newstead, and R. J. Olsen. 1985. Comparing public and private schools: The puzzling role of selectivity bias. *Journal of Business & Economic Statistics* 3:23–35.

Oakes, J. 1985. *Keeping track of how schools structure inequality.* New Haven: Yale University Press.

Partnership for Hope. 1991. *Pride and poverty: A report on San Antonio.* San Antonio, Tex.: Partnership for Hope.

Rubenstein, M., R. Hamar, and N. Adelman. 1992. *Minnesota's open enrollment option.* U. S. Department of Education Contract No. 89089001. Washington, D.C.: Policy Studies Associates.

Schmidt, Peter. 1994. Magnet's efficacy as a desegregation tool questioned. *Education Week,* February 2.

Tomas Rivera Center. 1993. *Resolving the crisis in education: Latino teachers for tomorrow's classrooms.* Claremont, Calif.: Tomas Rivera Center.

Willms, J. D. 1983. Do private schools produce higher levels of academic achievement? New evidence for the tuition tax credit debate. In T. James and H. M. Levin, eds., *Public dollars for private schools.* Philadelphia: Temple University Press.

Willms, J. D., and F. Echols. 1992. Alert and inert clients: The Scottish experience of parental choice of schools. *Economics of Education Review* 11:339–50.

Witte, J. and M. E. Rigdon. 1992. Private school choice: The Milwaukee low-income voucher experiment. Paper presented at the annual meeting of the American Political Science Association, September 2, in Chicago, Ill.

4

Private Vouchers in Indianapolis: The Golden Rule Program

MICHAEL HEISE,
KENNETH D. COLBURN JR., and
JOSEPH F. LAMBERTI

Introduction

The Educational Choice Charitable Trust, based in Indianapolis and created in 1991, is the nation's first large-scale, privately funded educational voucher program.[1] The trust is designed to provide a limited number of Indianapolis's low-income families with the same educational options that their more affluent counterparts enjoy. By providing tuition vouchers, the trust program increases low-income families' access to private schools. Increased access to private schools increases the families' choices about and control over where and how to educate their children. Because the trust program is funded entirely by private donations, difficult legal and regulatory issues concerning private schools that enroll trust-supported students are avoided.

Besides increasing the opportunity for more low-income families to attend private schools, the trust lets us observe how one type of school choice program operates and allows us to assess its efficacy. Although various types of school choice policies are the subject of increasing debate among educators, researchers, policy makers, and parents, the relative paucity of school choice programs restricts the availability of useful data. Data from the trust program provide valu-

The authors wish to acknowledge the helpful comments of Dennis E. Hinkle, dean, College of Education, Towson State University. This chapter also benefited from the research assistance of Wade Wingler and the administrative assistance of Katheryn Haines and Robin M. Polin.

able information about the effects of privately funded educational voucher programs. As a first step, it is important to examine who participates, why they do so, and the types of private schools they select. Data from the trust program, though preliminary, offer some valuable insights on these important questions.

This chapter, which presents descriptive data on the trust program's second year of operation, consists of three sections. The first section includes a description of the trust program and its development. The second section discusses the research design and methodology used in this study. The third section discusses the results, focusing on the demographic characteristics of participating and nonparticipating families, the reasons people participate in the trust program, and the private schools they select.

The Educational Choice
Charitable Trust Program

J. Patrick Rooney created the trust program, the nation's first large-scale privately funded educational voucher program. The trust is designed to increase a limited number of low-income families' access to private schools. Rooney, chairman of the Golden Rule Insurance Company, wanted to provide more low-income families the same opportunities enjoyed by wealthier families. In particular, Rooney felt that more low-income families deserved an opportunity to select the schools their children attend. As a visible presence in Indianapolis's corporate and Catholic communities, as well as one of a handful of white members of a predominantly African-American, inner-city parish, Rooney was aware of education's importance to children as well as the need to increase educational opportunities, particularly for children from less-affluent families.

Through the trust program, Rooney attempted to achieve two distinct goals. The explicit goal was to provide greater access to private schools for a limited number of children from low-income families. (Although trust grant recipients can send their children to any school located in Marion County—private or public—all have selected private schools.) A second implicit and subordinate goal was to assess the efficacy of private educational vouchers as an educational policy.

The trust provides grants to a limited number of low-income families that reside within the Indianapolis public school district and want to enroll their children in private elementary schools. In addition to the residency requirement, only families eligible for the federal reduced-fee lunch program can apply for trust funds. Participating families apply trust grants toward tuition at any private school, including religious schools, in Marion County. The trust allocates half its funds to families wanting to enroll their children in private schools for the first time. Eligible families whose children already attend private schools receive the remaining funds.

Rooney announced the trust program at a Friday afternoon press conference in mid-August 1991. Because the trust program was the first of its kind in the United States, the announcement attracted considerable media coverage. Trust officials received hundreds of calls for applications within seventy-two hours of the initial announcement. By the following Monday, trust officials had to create a waiting list to accommodate the strong demand.

The trust program is entirely privately funded. As a result, private schools enrolling trust-supported students are not subject to increased governmental regulation. The Golden Rule Insurance Company provided the initial capital, and several other corporations and individuals have contributed since. Originally designed to last for three school years, trust officials recently announced their intention of extending the program another two years. The trust's ability to raise funds is, obviously, directly associated with the number of families it is able to assist. During its second year the trust served 874 students in sixty different private schools.[2]

Local community centers, many private (particularly Catholic) schools, and the Golden Rule Insurance Company distribute grant applications. The early formation of a waiting list suggested to trust program officials that formal marketing and information outreach activities were not a priority. The trust's two-person staff instead focused its efforts on administration, fund raising, and other programmatic tasks. Indeed, only by increasing the trust's financial resources could the program attempt to reduce the size of its growing waiting list. As discussed below, however, the reliance on news coverage along with an informal dissemination effort by the Catholic schools' leadership played an important role in determining who heard about the trust program and when.

Parents applying for trust funds complete a two-page application, which they then take to the school of their choice where they formally apply for admission to that school. Administrators at private schools enrolling trust-supported students complete a one-page application that includes information about the school's tuition. Private school administrators must also certify that trust applicants meet the program's financial guidelines.

Once a private school accepts a trust program applicant, its administrators send the student's grant application to the program office. As the trust office receives completed applications, the program's executive director notifies private school administrators whether trust funds are available for an admitted student. Private school administrators then notify parents of the final decision. The trust awards grants on a first-come, first-served basis and does not consider any other criteria, such as student grades or behavior. Moreover, private schools maintain complete control over whom they enroll.

Two aspects of the trust program deserve note. First, the trust limits grants to half of a private school's tuition, up to $800 a student. Participating families pay for at least half of their child's private school tuition, regardless of what the private school charges (none of the private schools in this study are tuition free). The copayment requirement reflects two factors. One factor is that the trust program wants to provide a "helping hand" rather than a "handout." By requiring participating families to invest in their child's education, the trust hopes to encourage parental involvement in their children's education. Also, by limiting the size of its grants, the trust can extend its reach to a larger number of families.

A second important aspect of the program is its restriction to low-income families. Specifically, only families that qualify for the federal government's reduced-fee lunch program can participate. By focusing on low-income families, the trust is better able to achieve its goal of increasing access to private schools.

Along with increasing low-income families's access to private schools, the trust program provides important information about how privately funded educational voucher programs operate. Public and academic debates about the effects of privately funded voucher programs have increased in recent years as more policy makers consider an array of school choice options. Although an ample research literature exists on how educational vouchers might work in theory, Witte (1992) correctly points to a significant gap in the literature on what is known about how educational vouchers actually operate. A paucity of relevant data limits the public debate surrounding the educational voucher issue in particular and the school choice debate generally. The absence (until recently) of educational voucher programs certainly contributes to the paucity of data.

Proponents of educational vouchers (e.g., Chubb and Moe 1990; Sugarman 1974; Coons and Sugarman 1992) emphasize their desired effects, such as increased choice for consumers of educational services—families and their school-age children, particularly low-income families—as well as increased competition for providers of educational services, public and private schools. Critics of educational vouchers (e.g., Kozol 1991; Levin 1990), in contrast, argue that they will favor more-affluent and better-educated families and further erode support for public schools.

Many aspects of the educational voucher debate would benefit from more and better information on privately funded voucher programs' effects on students, families, and schools, public and private. In particular, it would be helpful to know more about who participates in these programs, why they participate, and what kinds of schools they select. Data from the trust program, though limited and preliminary, are among the first relating these and other important questions concerning privately funded educational vouchers, their effects, and their implications for policy.

Research Design and Methodology

To increase understanding about privately funded educational vouchers' effects on students, families, and schools, trust program participants and administrators at private schools enrolling trust-supported students are surveyed annually. The surveys incorporate many items developed by John Witte in his evaluation of the nation's only publicly funded educational voucher program, the Milwaukee Parental Choice Program (MPCP). The surveys focus on two broad questions, the first of which involves general demographic data on participating families, such as household income, race, marital status, and parental educational achievement. Selected demographic characteristics of the trust participants (as well as a subset of participants who left the Indianapolis public schools) are presented and compared with those of nonchoosing households with school-age children living within the public school district boundaries.

A second question addressed by the survey explores motivations for trust program participants and the types of schools they select. Data on these issues help assess whether those who participate in educational voucher programs do so for education-related reasons or for other reasons. These data are presented for various groups of parents: those whose children attended private schools before receiving trust funds (labeled "private" in the following analysis); those whose children switched from public to private schools during the first year of the trust program ("privpub, exit year one"); those whose children switched from public to private schools during the second year of the trust program ("privpub, exit year two"); and those whose children applied for and were accepted into the trust program but remain on a waiting list and in public schools because of limited funds ("waitlist").

Because children from families in the waitlist group remain in public schools, comparisons of these families with groups of parents whose children now attend private schools as a result of the trust program are particularly informative. Much of the existing research on the effects of educational vouchers (both publicly and privately funded) is criticized partly for the absence of an adequate control group. This absence makes it difficult to assess the independent effects of choosing to participate in a voucher program and attending a private school because families inclined to participate in a school voucher program may fundamentally differ from families not so inclined and whose children remain in public schools. Therefore, the trust program's waiting list serves as a crude control group, providing a subset of families and children similar to active participants in that they qualify for and have elected to participate in the trust program. The salient difference, of course, is that those on the waiting list remain in Indianapolis public schools solely as a result of the program's limited funds.

During the program's second year (1992–93) 1,064 surveys were mailed to participating parents. Of these, 465 went to parents in the private group; 409 to the privpub group; and 190 to parents in the waitlist group. The surveys' overall response rate was 53 percent. In addition, principals at the sixty private schools enrolling trust grant recipients received administrator surveys. Schools that failed to respond to our written surveys received up to three follow-up telephone calls. Sixty-six percent of the surveyed principals responded.

It is important to note a few limitations to the data discussed below. First, the evaluation of the trust program has not yet reached its midpoint. Accordingly, the data discussed below are preliminary, the analyses descriptive. Second, although the survey response rates in this study compare favorably with those of similar, ongoing research efforts, it is possible that nonrespondents may systematically differ from those who did respond. Limitations aside, however, these data are among the earliest generated by the nation's first and one of its largest privately funded educational voucher programs.

Along with the trust program, two other large-scale privately funded educational voucher programs currently operate in the United States: the Children's Educational Opportunity (CEO) Foundation, operating in San Antonio, and the Partners Advancing Values in Education (PAVE), operating in Milwaukee. Both programs are modeled after the trust program and therefore share many important characteristics. Because all three of the nation's privately funded voucher programs resemble one another, comparisons of findings are included where appropriate.

Results and Discussion

DEMOGRAPHIC CHARACTERISTICS OF PARTICIPATING FAMILIES

One key question surrounding the school choice debate involves what type of family is likely to participate in an educational voucher program. Of particular interest is whether participating families are wealthier, better educated, or more stable than families that elect not to particpate and whose children remain in public schools. Critics of school choice policies assert that educational voucher programs lure away the most educable children and relegate to public schools an even greater concentration of children with more demanding educational needs (see e.g., Kozol 1991). Although the trust program's size and scope are limited, preliminary data from its second year of operation offer useful information on these questions.

To develop a broad demographic decription of trust program participants, selected data from participating families (private and privpub) are compared with

Table 1   Income Levels of Participating Families (%)

Income ($)	Private [a] (n=180)	Privpub [b] (n=167)	Indianapolis Public Schools [c] (households with children) (1990 census)
0–4,999	9.4	13.2	9.5
5,000–9,999	13.3	10.2	9.4
10,000–14,999	21.1	26.9	10.6
15,000–19,999	23.9	22.8	9.9
20,000–24,999	18.3	15.6	9.9
25,000–29,999	5.6	6.0	9.8
30,000–34,999	5.6	4.2	8.4
35,000 and above	2.8	0.6	32.5

[a] Choice trust participants from private schools.
[b] Choice trust participants who left public for private schools.
[c] Households with school-age children residing in Indianapolis School District.

census data from nonparticipants, that is, households with school-age children (ages three to nineteen) within the Indianapolis public school district.[3] Two major findings emerge from the data presented in tables 1 and 2. One is that the similarities between participating and nonparticipating families generally outnumber the differences. Second, trust program participants are generally similar to their counterparts in the privately funded voucher programs in Milwaukee and San Antonio.

Household Income.   The trust program is limited to families whose income qualifies them for the federal reduced-fee lunch program. This income restriction reduces the importance of income as a variable because it substantially limits variation in income. What variation does exist, however, warrants discussion.

We expected and found that participating family income levels are far below income levels for Indianapolis public school families. Our expectations were influenced by one main factor: Only families whose income qualifies them for the federal reduced-fee lunch program are eligible to receive a trust grant. This requirement exerts downward pressure on participating family income. In contrast, public school family income data include all households with children residing in Indianapolis school district boundaries. The inclusion of the public school data of income information on all rather than low-income families exerts upward pressure on income levels.

The household income data presented in table 1 illustrate that the trust program achieves its goal of increasing educational options for low-income

Table 2   Demographics of Parents of Indianapolis Schoolchildren

			INDIANAPOLIS PUBLIC SCHOOLS	
	Private [a] *(%)*	*Privpub* [b] *(%)*	*Public* [c] *(%)*	*Private* [d] *(%)*
Married (includes all remarried)	48	47	54	—
Not married (includes single, divorced)	52	53	46	—
Less than high school	9	9	34	—
High school or General Equivalency Diploma	37	34	32	—
Some college	42	48	24	—
College and more	12	9	10	—
RACIAL IDENTITY OF CHILDREN				
African American	35	56	53	25
White	59	37	45	73
Hispanic	2	3	2	2
Other	4	4	1	1

[a] Choice trust participants from private schools.
[b] Choice trust participants who left public for private schools.
[c] Indianapolis households with children attending public schools.
[d] Indianapolis households with children attending private schools.

families. For example, approximately 70 percent of the participating families report an income level under $20,000. About 23 percent report incomes of less than $10,000. Because of the trust program's household income restriction, it is impossible to discern from these data whether the program is particularly attractive to families at either end of the income spectrum. That approximately 23 percent of the participating families report earning less than $10,000, however, suggests that low-income families are responsive and drawn to the program. The data also indicate the private families are better off financially than privpub families. Because of the cost of private school tuition, it is not surprising to find that children from families in the higher end of the low-income spectrum are more likely to have attended private schools before their participation in the trust program.

Marital Status. The trust program attracts a higher than expected percentage of children from households headed by a single parent—more than half (see table 2). In contrast, one-parent families head 46 percent of nonparticipating households.

Participants' marital status might relate to their household income. Because two-parent households typically earn more than single-head households, two-parent families are less likely to meet the trust program's income requirements. Household income's correlation with marital status makes it difficult to discern reasons for the program's popularity among single-parent families. Regardless of the underlying reason, however, these data suggest that the trust reaches a disproportionate number of children from single-parent households.

Racial and Ethnic Origin.   One of the more important topics surrounding the general debate about educational vouchers is their potential impact on racial and ethnic school integration (Plank 1993). An important component of this larger question is whether whites are more likely than nonwhites to participate in a voucher program. Data presented in table 2 suggest two important and potentially related findings. First, the percentage of nonwhite students in the privpub group exceeds the percentage of nonwhite students in the nonparticipating pool of public school students. For example, the percentage of African-American students in the privpub group (56) exceeds the percentage of African-American students attending public schools (53). Second, the percentage of nonwhite students in the private group (41) exceeds the percentage of nonwhite students attending private schools in the public school district (27). Notwithstanding the importance of the data in table 2, note that the pool of nonparticipating IPS students includes all students, not just low-income students. A different contrast would probably emerge if the nonparticipating pool of public school students included only those from low-income families.

Parental Educational Attainment.   Data on parental educational attainment suggest that parents with more formal education are more likely to participate in the trust program (see table 2). This finding supports some criticisms of educational voucher programs and is generally consistent with similar data from other privately funded voucher programs.

The percentage of nonparticipating Indianapolis public school households (from all income groups) headed by a parent lacking a high school diploma (34) noticeably exceeds corresponding percentages for both groups of parents participating in the trust program. That the groups of trust parents include only low-income families, in contrast to the IPS data, makes differences between IPS and trust data even more striking. Assuming that wealthier parents tend to complete more education, the educational attainment differences between a subset of low-income IPS families and families participating in the trust program presumably would be even greater.

One explanation for the findings in table 2 is that more highly educated parents might place a higher value on the importance of education for their children. These parents might also be more motivated to respond quickly to opportunities such as those created by the trust program. Another explanation involves the relative abilities of parents with varying levels of educational attainment to respond to the opportunity presented by the trust program. Because the trust serves a limited number of students and grants are awarded on a first-come, first-serve basis, parents desiring private education and able to respond quickly gain an important advantage. Therefore, it might be that parents with more education are better able to seek out and act on information about the trust program than parents with less formal education. These less-educated parents might be equally attracted to the trust program and simply have responded later.

A second, though less important, finding relates to the approximately 9 percent of participating parents that report graduating from college (see table 2). This aspect is surprising considering that these college graduates report earning incomes that qualify them for the federal reduced-fee lunch program.

The overall impression created by the demographic data in tables 1 and 2 is mixed. That is, educational voucher advocates and critics will both find empirical support. Nevertheless, it appears that the trust program is achieving its goals. Specifically, the program increases educational opportunities for a limited number of low-income families by increasing their access to and choice of private schools. By design, the program reaches its intended audience: low-income families. At the same time, the program reaches a disproportionate number of children from single-parent families as well as from racial and ethnic minorities. The trust program attracts parents with relatively higher educational levels. Whether this finding reflects issues such as access to information about the program or the ability to respond to educational opportunities, as opposed to parental commitment to increasing educational opportunities for their children, remains unclear.

REASONS FOR PARTICIPATING AND SCHOOLS SELECTED

A second group of survey questions focuses on why parents participate in the trust program and which private schools they select for their children. An important question in many school choice policy debates is whether families seek schools for reasons of convenience rather than, for example, concerns about educational quality. Also, how parents learn about the trust program is particularly important because the parents' source of information appears to influence when they learn about the availability of trust grants. Finally, an examination of the characteristics of the selected private schools may shed some light on the aspects of schooling that participating families find important.

To learn more about the issues addressed by these questions, we organized the data in tables 3 and 4 into three groups. Along with the private (families whose children already attended private schools before receiving a trust grant) and privpub (families whose children exited Indianapolis public schools for private schools as a result of trust grants) groups discussed above, we also include data on the waitlist group. That group includes parents whose children applied

Table 3   How Parents Learned about the Program (%)

	News-paper	TV and Radio	Friends and Relatives	Church	Private School	(N)
FIRST SOURCE [a]						
Private [b]	22.9	13.1	22.1	14.3	28	175
Privpub [c]	23.8	8.9	32.7	8.9	24.4	168
Waitlist [d]	10.8	11.8	39.2	7.8	29.4	102
SECOND SOURCE						
Private	1.5	15.2	36.4	15.2	25.8	66
Privpub	0	29.5	27.3	11.4	22.7	44
Waitlist	0	23.1	30.8	0	34.6	26
PARENT/GUARDIAN EDUCATIONAL LEVEL						
Less than high school	19.2	7.7	21.2	19.2	30.8	52
High school (or General Equivalency Diploma)	17.6	9.8	28.8	9.8	33.3	153
Some college	18.4	13.5	33.8	10.1	22.7	207
College (or more)	46.2	7.7	17.9	7.7	20.5	29

[a] Question: "How did you originally learn about the Educational Choice Charitable Trust Program? (Check all that apply)"

[b] Choice trust participants from private schools.

[c] Choice trust participants who left public for private schools.

[d] Parents on choice trust waiting list whose children remain in public schools.

for and were accepted into the trust program but remain on a waiting list and attend public schools. We then divided the privpub group into two different subgroups: privpub, exit year one and privpub, exit year two (see tables 5 and 6). This designation distinguishes parents that switched from public to private schools in year one from those that switched in year two, which is important for survey questions asking respondents to reflect on the previous school year (1991–92). Those in the privpub, exit year one, group reflect on private schools; those in the privpub, exit year two, group, on public schools.

As discussed previously, a common criticism of research comparing the effects of educational voucher programs frequently focuses on the absence of an adequate control group. Therefore, the importance of the waitlist bears repeating. The two groups of participating parents (private and privpub) resemble those in the waitlist group in that parents from all groups applied for and were accepted into the trust program. The crucial difference is that children of waitlist parents continue to attend Indianapolis public schools. This difference stems from the

Table 4   Reasons for Participating in Choice Program (%)

	Very Important	Important	Somewhat Important	Not Important	(N)
Educational quality					
Private [a]	89	11	0	0	182
Privpub [b]	91.2	8.8	0	0	170
Waitlist [c]	95.1	4.9	0	0	103
Safety					
Private	84.0	16.0	0	0	181
Privpub	86.5	13.5	0	0	170
Waitlist	88.2	11.8	0	0	102
Financial considerations					
Private	77.8	16.7	5.6	0	180
Privpub	78.8	17.1	4.1	0	170
Waitlist	78.4	18.6	2.9	0	102
General atmosphere					
Private	77.7	22.3	0	0	179
Privpub	82.1	17.3	0	0	108
Waitlist	81.2	18.8	0	0	101
Availability of program					
Private	72	28	0	0	182
Privpub	74.4	25.6	0	0	168
Waitlist	78.4	21.6	0	0	102
Discipline					
Private	73.6	23.1	3.3	0	182
Privpub	71.9	25.7	2.3	0	171
Waitlist	75.2	20.8	4.0	0	101
Religious values					
Private	78.5	18.2	3.3	0	181
Privpub	71.3	21.1	7.6	0	171
Waitlist	70.6	20.6	8.8	0	102
Location					
Private	57.5	28.2	10.5	3.9	181
Privpub	55.6	29	4.2	4.1	109
Waitlist	69.3	20.8	5.9	4.0	101

[a] Choice trust participants from private schools.
[b] Choice trust participants who left public for private schools.
[c] Parents on choice trust waiting list whose children remain in public schools.

Table 4   (continued)

	Very Important	Important	Somewhat Important	Not Important	(N)
Frustration with public schools					
Private [a]	59.9	18.6	12.8	8.7	172
Privpub [b]	59.3	26.5	7.4	6.8	162
Waitlist [c]	65.3	18.8	8.9	6.9	101
Special programs					
Private	54.4	31.7	6.7	7.2	180
Privpub	56.2	30.8	8.3	4.7	169
Waitlist	56.4	29.7	8.9	5.0	101
Siblings in chosen school					
Private	37.3	32.2	13.6	16.9	177
Privpub	31.9	31.9	16.6	19.6	163
Waitlist	36.4	33.3	17.2	13.1	99

[a] Choice trust participants from private schools.
[b] Choice trust participants who left public for private schools.
[c] Parents on choice trust waiting list whose children remain in public schools.

trust program's limited resources. By controlling somewhat for possible selection bias, the waitlist group can serve as a crude proxy for a control group.

How Parents Learn about the Trust Program.   How participating parents learn about the trust program is consequential for two reasons. First, the program's first-come, first-serve basis for awarding grants favors parents who learn about the program early. Second, as previously discussed, the trust program does not pursue a formal outreach or dissemination strategy. As a result, the importance of alternative information dissemination mechanisms increases. These alternative mechanisms include word of mouth, the media, religious institutions, and private schools. Different groups report learning about the trust program from different sources. This variation is important because those on the waiting list presumably heard about the trust program later than those in the other groups (private and privpub).

Data suggest that newspapers and, to a lesser extent, churches were among the timely ways to learn about the trust program (see table 3). The relative importance of churches as sources of information about the trust program can be attributed largely to a coordinated effort by Indianapolis's Catholic diocesan to promote and disseminate information about the trust program. The diocesan's incentive—to increase Catholic school enrollment—is clear. As discussed below,

Table 5   Parent/Guardian Satisfaction with Last Year's School (%)

	Satisfied	Dissatisfied	(N)
Location			
Private [a]	97	3	231
Privpub, exit year 1 [b]	95.8	4.2	95
Privpub, exit year 2 [c]	84.8	15.2	99
Waitlist [d]	79.4	20.6	102
Child's safety			
Private	95.7	4.3	231
Privpub, exit year 1	92.6	7.4	95
Privpub, exit year 2	82.8	17.2	99
Waitlist	77.2	22.8	101
Program of instruction			
Private	96.1	3.9	231
Privpub, exit year 1	89.5	10.5	94
Privpub, exit year 2	77.6	22.4	98
Waitlist	67.6	32.4	102
School academic standards			
Private	96.1	3.9	229
Privpub, exit year 1	92.6	7.4	94
Privpub, exit year 2	83.5	16.5	97
Waitlist	66.7	33.3	99
Opportunity for parental involvement			
Private	94.4	5.6	231
Privpub, exit year 1	96.8	3.2	94
Privpub, exit year 2	80.6	19.4	98
Waitlist	80	20	100
Amount child learned			
Private	93.5	6.5	231
Privpub, exit year 1	89.4	10.6	94
Privpub, exit year 2	79.6	20.4	98
Waitlist	63.7	36.3	102
Principal's performance			
Private	86.6	13.4	231
Privpub, exit year 1	88.5	11.5	96
Privpub, exit year 2	81.1	18.9	95
Waitlist	71	29	100

[a] Choice trust participants from private schools.
[b] Choice trust participants who left public for private schools during the first year of the program.
[c] Choice trust participants who left public for private schools during the second year of the program.
[d] Parents on choice trust waiting list whose children remain in public schools.

Table 5   (*continued*)

	Satisfied	Dissatisfied	(N)
Discipline			
Private [a]	91.3	8.7	231
Privpub, exit year 1 [b]	89.5	10.5	95
Privpub, exit year 2 [c]	73.7	26.3	99
Waitlist [d]	63.4	36.6	101
Opportunity for parents to influence school policy			
Private	88.7	11.3	231
Privpub, exit year 1	92.6	6.4	94
Privpub, exit year 2	69.5	30.5	95
Waitlist	57	43	100
Value of homework			
Private	93.9	6.1	229
Privpub, exit year 1	91.6	8.4	95
Privpub, exit year 2	83	17	94
Waitlist	66.3	33.7	95
Teacher's performance			
Private	91.3	8.3	229
Privpub, exit year 1	88.5	10.4	96
Privpub, exit year 2	79.8	20.2	99
Waitlist	67.3	32.7	101

[a] Choice trust participants from private schools.
[b] Choice trust participants who left public for private schools during the first year of the program.
[c] Choice trust participants who left public for private schools during the second year of the program.
[d] Parents on choice trust waiting list whose children remain in public schools.

the number of trust recipients attending Catholic schools reflects the diocesan's efforts.

Two other sources of information about the trust program warrant note as they are frequently cited by all families, particularly those on the waiting list. The waitlist group disproportionately cites families and friends as well as private schools as sources of information. The sources' popularity among waitlist families suggests that they were not as timely as other potential sources.

Why Parents Participate.   Just as important as how parents learn about the trust program are their reasons for participating. Reasons that parents report as important, as well as those they describe as less important, offer clues about what parents look for in the schools their children attend. Data on parents' motivations

Table 6   Parent/Guardian Grades for Child's School Last Year (%)

	A	B	C	D	F	(N)
Private [a]	41.2	37.7	18	1.8	1.3	228
Privpub, exit year 1 [b]	48.4	29	14	8.6	0	93
Privpub, exit year 2 [c]	34	35	17	7	7	100
Waitlist [d]	20.6	25.8	30.9	16.5	6.2	97

[a] Choice trust participants from private schools.
[b] Choice trust participants who left public for private schools during the first year of the program.
[c] Choice trust participants who left public for private schools during the second year of the program.
[d] Parents on choice trust waiting list whose children remain in public schools.

for participating in the privately funded school voucher program are especially important, in part because of criticisms relating to nonacademic motivations. Specifically, many school voucher critics assert that participating parents, particularly low-income parents, place higher priority on reasons other than the academic quality of a school. For example, in its school choice study, the Carnegie Corporation (1992) concluded that parents who participate in school choice programs do so mostly for nonacademic reasons. Data from the trust program, however, do not support such a conclusion (see table 4).

As these data make clear, foremost among the reasons parents participate in the trust is educational quality, with more than 90 percent describing educational quality as "very important." Other factors that more than 70 percent of participating parents describe as very important include financial considerations, school safety, general atmosphere and religious values of the selected school, and discipline.

Equally informative are the reasons parents describe as relatively less important, including factors such as school location and where other children attended school (see table 4). This finding evidences parents' willingness to endure possible inconveniences to take advantage of greater educational opportunity.

The general absence of significant frustration with Indianapolis public schools voiced by those parents whose children left public schools is another interesting finding (see table 5). Parents in the private and privpub, exit year one, groups are reflecting on private schools. In contrast, those in the privpub, exit year two, and waitlist groups are reflecting on their satisfaction with the public schools. Data from all four groups are generally consistent with data presented in table 4 and underscore two main points.

First, private schools satisfy parents more than public schools. Specifically, satisfaction levels for the private and privpub, exit year one, groups exceed that of the other two groups on every survey item. Moreover, among those describing private schools, higher satisfaction is reported generally by those who have attended private schools for more than one year. What is suggested is that satisfaction with private schools increases with over time.

Second, parents from all groups report relatively high satisfaction levels. All parents on all items report being more satisfied than not with different aspects of the schools their children attended during 1991–92. This finding is particularly notable for the two groups of parents describing Indianapolis public schools (privpub, exit year two, and waitlist).

The two themes suggested by the satisfaction data in table 5—that parents are generally satisfied, particularly with private schools—are also suggested by the grades parents assign to the schools their children attended during the prior year. Private schools received higher grades than those received by IPS schools (see table 6). In addition, all schools, even the public schools, received relatively high grades for performance. For example, more than 46 percent of the waitlist group felt that the performance of their children's public school during the 1991–92 school year warranted an A or B.

Characteristics of the Private School Selected. Although data from surveys of participating parents do not reveal profound dissatisfaction with the overall quality of the educational services provided by the Indianapolis public schools, that participating parents choose to exit those schools evidences some level of preference for private schools. (The waiting list of additional parents who want to leave public for private schools also suggests a preference for private schools.) Participating families use trust funds at any private school located in the district.

An analysis of selected schools identifies attributes that parents seek in schools. During the trust program's second year of operation, 60 of the approximately 160 private schools located within the Indianapolis public school district enrolled trust-supported students. Of these, approximately two-thirds (n=40) responded to our survey. Data from this survey reveal two notable findings.

The first finding involves the influence of religious school. More than 80 percent of the responding schools are religiously affiliated. Of these religious schools, about 50 percent (n=15) are Catholic. Although Catholic schools account for just under half the total number of schools selected by trust parents, Catholic schools enroll more than 65 percent of the trust students. Catholic schools' domination of the trust program is not surprising as these schools are more numerous, larger, and more established in Indianapolis than other groups of private schools. Also, as described earlier, the Catholic schools actively promote the trust program to potential participants. Finally, the trust program's founder, J. Patrick Rooney, is a prominent and visible leader in Indianapolis's Catholic community.

A second notable finding is that most parents selected private schools located in what many would consider inner-city neighborhoods. This is partly a result of the popularity of Catholic schools and their location in many Indianapolis neighborhoods. Accordingly, 82 percent of those attending Catholic schools do so in one of Indianapolis's core neighborhoods. Because many of the non-Catholic private schools are also located in Indianapolis, most (79 percent) students attending non-Catholic schools also do so in Indianapolis's downtown area. This finding suggests that many parents are more concerned with sending their children to higher-performing local schools rather than to schools in nonurban neighborhoods.

Conclusion

The trust program provides a limited number of low-income families with an opportunity already enjoyed by wealthier families: to select and attend a private school. The program also provides researchers and policy makers important data from the nation's first large-scale privately funded voucher program. Although little can be reasonably concluded from these preliminary data, they present crucial though incomplete information on important questions surrounding privately funded educational voucher programs in particular and school choice policies in general. These questions concern the types of families who participate in the trust program, why they participate, and the private schools they select. These questions are central to the growing public policy debate surrounding school choice.

The data suggest that the trust program is reaching its goal of reducing the financial barrier to the private school market for a limited number of low-income families. Moreover, in comparison to all families with school-age children living within Indianapolis's boundaries, students participating in the trust program are disproportionately nonwhite and come from single-head households. Concern about school quality is the most important reason parents participate. Religiously affiliated schools, particularly parochial schools, attract most trust-supported students.

Although the weight of the evidence suggests that the trust program appears to be meeting its goal, the data also identify potential problems with certain aspects of the trust program and do not address other important questions relating to the school choice debate. One potential problem involves information about the trust program. Program participants learned about the availability of trust grants from a variety of sources. As a result, information reached different people at different times. Because demand for trust grants exceeds supply and grants are allocated to eligible families on a first-come, first-served basis, those families that learned about the availability of grants early gained an important advantage. A related point about information concerns the private schools. Specifically, there was no coordinated effort designed to disseminate information about private schools to participating families.

A second possible problem involves the educational levels of the parents of children receiving trust grants. In contrast to nonparticipating parents, parents in the trust program tend to be more highly educated. As a result, the trust program might not be reaching the least advantaged among the eligible low-income families. Instead, the trust program might reach those low-income families who were already inclined toward private schools but unable to afford full tuition. Although the program is not designed to distinguish among different levels of parental education within low-income families, children of parents with relatively lower educational levels would also benefit from trust grants.

Although these data are helpful, important questions about the efficacy of educational vouchers remain. Perhaps most important is their effect on student academic achievement, in particular, whether participation in the trust program results in students learning more or even perhaps learning at the same rate but in a more cost-effective manner. Implications for public and private schools also warrant attention. Although the trust program serves fewer than one thousand students, it operates without jeopardizing the integrity of the public school system. Indeed, a vibrant system of public and private schools only increases parental options regarding education for their children. The trust program's limited size and scope (grants are capped at $800 a student) suppress the development of new private schools. However, the supply-side effects of a larger voucher system are unclear. Finally, because the trust funds are private, private schools receiving grant-supported students are not encumbered with governmental regulation or loss of autonomy. Implications for private schools posed by increased governmental regulation that would likely accompany publicly funded educational vouchers deserve close analysis.

Overall results from this preliminary analysis of the trust program provide an important initial glimpse into how larger educational vouchers and school choice programs might operate, who would participate, their reasons for doing so, and the types of schools they would select. These data also illustrate how educational voucher programs can be designed to reach those most in need of greater school choice and more effective educational services.

Notes

1. Research for this chapter was supported in part by Grant No. 920525 from the Lilly Endowment, Inc.

2. This analysis considers only data from the trust program's second year of operation (1992–93). Data from the second year are the most recent available and include information on students and families who remain on the trust program's waiting list.

3. U.S. Dept. of Education, National Center for Education Statistics, 1990 Census School District Special Tabulation, Summary File Set I (11/93). Data supplied from the 1990 U.S. Census by the U.S. Department of Commerce, Bureau of Census.

References

Carnegie Corporation for the Advancement of Teaching. *School Choice*. Princeton, N.J.: Carnegie Corporation for the Advancement of Teaching, 1992.

Chubb, John E., and Terry M. Moe. *Politics, Markets, and American Schools*. Washington, D.C.: Brookings Institution, 1990.

Coons, John E., and Stephen E. Sugarman. *Scholarships for Children*. Berkeley: University of California Press, 1992.

Kozol, Jonathan. *Savage Inequalities*. New York: Crown Books, 1991.

Levine, Gail F. "Meeting the Third Wave: Legislative Approaches to Recent Judicial School Finance Rulings." *Harvard Journal on Legislation* 28 (1991): 507.

Plank, Stephen, et al. "Effects of Choice in Education." In Edith Rasell and Richard Rothstein, eds., *School Choice: Examining the Evidence*. Washington, D.C.: Economic Policy Institute, 1993.

Sugarman, Stephen D. "Family Choice: The Next Step in the Quest for Equal Educational Opportunity?" *Law and Contemporary Problems* 38 (1974): 513–65.

Witte, John F. "Public Subsidies for Private Schools: What We Know and How to Proceed." *Educational Policy* 6, no. 2 (1992): 206–27.

5

Private Vouchers in New York City: The Student-Sponsor Partnership Program

PAUL T. HILL

One of the country's largest and oldest private voucher programs, New York City's Student-Sponsor Partnership Program, offers a second chance at education for hundreds of low-income minority high school students. It was founded by Peter Flanigan, a New York City investment banker who had worked for many years to improve educational opportunities for low-income and minority city youth. As an early sponsor of Eugene Lang's "I Have a Dream Program," Flanigan had adopted a class of public elementary school students and promised to pay college tuition for any that finished high school and qualified for higher education. Like many other "I Have a Dream" sponsors, Flanigan became disillusioned with the public schools as he helped his adoptees struggle through impersonal and chaotic middle and high schools. Convinced that there had to be an alternative to such schools, he decided to try placing students in some of New York City's low-cost Catholic high schools. He and a group of other professionals from New York law and investment firms identified at-risk students, negotiated their placement in Catholic high schools, and promised to pay the tuition bills.

The program enrolled its first students in September 1986. Now, eight years later, Flanigan and a small paid staff assemble donations from hundreds of private individuals and use the funds to pay tuition in private, mostly Catholic, high schools. A total of 535 sponsors pay tuition averaging $2,750 in fifteen inner-city high schools. The program has placed more than 1,300 students in private schools since 1986. Through the 1993–94 school year, 483 of its students have

Table 1   Demographic Characteristics of Partnership versus NYC Public
           School Students 1986–95

	Percentage of Partnership Student Population	*Percentage of NYC Public School Population*
African-American	60	39
Hispanic	35	36
Male	55	50
Family on welfare	60	na[a]
From single-parent home	76	na
Lives with neither parent	14	na

[a] na = not available.
SOURCE: Student-Sponsor Partnership Program

Table 2   Sources of New Partnership Students

Person or Organization Referring Students	*(%)*
Public school teacher or counselor	57
Community-based organization	13
Partnership school	9
Church	4
Self-nominated	17

SOURCE: Student-Sponsor Partnership Program

graduated from high school, and 837 are in high school during the 1994–95
academic year.

The Student-Sponsor Partnership Program expressly seeks students who are
minority, low income, threatened by family and neighborhood problems, and
struggling in school. Partnership students are poorer and more heavily minority
than New York City high school students on average, and their rates of welfare
dependency are about average for students in the public high schools serving the
lowest-income students (see table 1).

Program recruiters find students by talking to public junior high school
guidance counselors, welfare and corrections officials, community-based organization staffs, youth center workers, and pastors, both Protestant and Catholic (see
table 2).

Before entering the program, students must be attending public junior high
or middle schools. The vast majority of students selected are achieving at or below
the average for the poverty-area junior high schools they attend, and many are in

Table 3   Test Scores for 1993 Incoming Partnership Students

	Reading	Mathematics
Grade equivalent		
Mean	66	7.9
Range	52–9.9	6.6–9.0
Percentile		
Mean	36	36
Range	11–60	25–50

SOURCE: Student-Sponsor Partnership Program

danger of dropping out. Although few Catholic schools can serve students with severe mental or emotional handicaps, they do accept private voucher students who are educationally disadvantaged by any measure. Partnership students admitted to ninth grade in 1993 performed well below grade level on both reading and mathematics (see table 3).

From 1989 through 1991, the author headed a RAND study of students who received vouchers from the program and the schools that served them. The research team wanted to know why, as appeared to be the case from raw data provided by the program, Partnership students were doing far better in private schools than they had been doing in public school. RAND compared the educational experiences of private voucher students with public school students in the same neighborhoods. The study report, *High Schools with Character* (Hill et al. 1991), also compares Partnership and public students' dropout and graduation rates, test scores, and college admission experience.

The Partnership private voucher program was a promising subject for research because the students were not self-selected or "creamed" off the top of the public school system; they were typical public school students who had not previously tried to attend private schools. They were also placed in extremely simple and low-cost private schools, not schools that were so lavishly staffed and funded that public schools could not hope to imitate them. The private schools participating in the program had only half to two-thirds of the New York City public schools' per pupil funding, and they had student-teacher ratios of twenty to one, much higher than the nearby public high schools' ratios of fifteen to one.

The study results confirmed the Partnership program's initial impression that its students were doing unusually well. In 1990, the last year of the RAND study, graduation rates for private voucher students were more than half again higher than New York City public high school students and nearly as high as the tuition-paying students in the Catholic schools they attended. For a comparison of the most recent four-year graduation rates for Partnership students, students in all

Table 4   Four-Year Graduation Rates, 1990–94

Student Groups	(%)
Partnership students	69
All New York City public high school students	39
Students from public high schools most Partnership students would have attended	29

SOURCE: Student-Sponsor Partnership Program; City of New York Office of the Comptroller

Table 5   Comparative Performance of Graduating Seniors in Public and Partnership Schools, 1990

Schools	Students Taking the SAT (%)	Average Combined SAT Score	Above Mean for African Americans (%)
Public	33	642	<30
Catholic			
Partnership students	85	803	>60
All students	85	815	>60

SOURCE: Student-Sponsor Partnership Program; New York City Board of Education

New York City high schools, and students in public high schools that most partnership students would have attended, see table 4.

For the RAND study, we compared the 1990 Scholastic Aptitude Test (SAT) scores of Partnership students with the scores of students in the public schools. The vast majority of private voucher students graduating from the Catholic schools take the SAT, which is required for admission to most selective colleges and universities; less than one-third of their peers in public high schools do so. Despite the fact that public school students taking the SAT were a select group, Partnership students' score were much higher. Although all the scores in table 5 are below the national average for all students, the scores for Partnership students are well above average for the most similar national norm group, all African-American students. Mean scores for all New York City students fall far below the national average for African-American students. Private voucher students scored nearly as well as their tuition-paying Catholic school classmates.

Partnership private voucher students' advantages extend to college admission and completion. Since the first Partnership graduating class in 1990, an average of 90 percent of participating students has attended college; of those attending college 90 percent have enrolled in four-year bachelor's degree–granting institutions directly out of high school. The first Partnership class, which graduated from high school in 1990, sent thirty-three of its thirty-nine graduates (85 percent) directly to college, and twenty graduated with bachelor's degrees only four years later—a graduation rate higher than that of the vast majority of public four-year colleges and universities.

These data confirm findings by Coleman (1982) and Bryk and Lee (1993) that Catholic high schools weaken the usual correlation between students' race or income and academic achievement. They show further that the educational experience in such schools works for students who are not Catholic and whose parents had never considered themselves well enough off to pay private school tuition.

The RAND study was, however, designed to do more than simply keep score between private and public schools. Its ultimate goal was to understand why private voucher programs for at-risk students work: what do students experience in the school that vouchers let them attend; how does the school program motivate and inform such students; and how do the adults who work in the school organize themselves to deliver the program?

Based on a detailed study of Partnership schools and a demographically matched set of nearby comprehensive public high schools, the research team concluded that the two kinds of schools were profoundly different. The schools that private voucher students attended stood for something: they were organizations dedicated to motivating and influencing children and to producing graduates who were ready for higher education, productive work, and effective citizenship. The public high schools in the neighborhoods where Partnership students lived were public bureaucracies, designed to ensure that public funds were properly spent, regulations followed, legislative mandates observed, and the civil service rights of workers respected. Although many teachers and administrators in the public schools cared deeply about students, the institutional environment of public education was dutiful, routinized, and impersonal. Public schools delivered instructional programs, but they seldom made aggressive efforts to change students' values and motivations—something that the private schools considered the core of their educational mission.

The differences between the schools attended by the Partnership's private voucher students and the public schools those children would have attended can be summarized under two headings: institutional independence and choice.

The Advantages of Institutional Independence

The private voucher schools have attributes as organizations that set them apart from the New York City public schools. Because they are independent, and thus not heavily regulated, they are, in effect, owned and operated by the people who work in them.

Private voucher schools operate as problem-solving organizations, taking the initiative to change their programs in response to emerging needs. If graduates are not measuring up to the school's standards, or if the needs of external clienteles such as employers and college admissions officers change, school leaders know they must change their methods. In contrast, comprehensive neighborhood schools are powerfully constrained by external mandates and rigid internal divisions of labor. Course offerings, limited by state and local curriculum mandates and teacher contracts, are difficult to change. School leaders, lacking the freedom to solve problems, often perceive themselves as not responsible for the results.

Private voucher schools protect and sustain their distinctive character, both by hiring staff members who accept the school's premises and by socializing new staff members. Drawing from the same pool of teachers who staff the public schools, they cannot always get the very best. But their clear missions and public images help discourage uncooperative staff members from applying and provide a definite basis for selecting and influencing new teachers and administrators. Public schools have no grounds, other than training and experience, to choose among applicants and no well-defined basis on which to influence the attitudes or behavior of new staff members.

Private voucher schools consider themselves accountable to the people who depend on their performance—parents, students, neighborhood and parish groups. Public schools answer primarily to bureaucratic superiors—outside rule-making, auditing, and assessment organizations.

The private voucher schools' organizational independence has important implications for the instruction and students' relationships with faculty, including:

Private voucher schools concentrate on student outcomes before all other matters. Those outcomes are meaningful in the real world, stated in terms of graduates' ability to succeed in adult studies and occupations, not simply in terms of course completion or test scores. Public schools focus primarily on delivering programs and following procedures.

Private voucher schools have strong social contracts that communicate the reciprocal responsibilities of administration, students, and teachers and establish the benefits that each derives from fulfilling the contract faithfully. These contracts make clear what opportunities the school promises to provide, what work and achievement is required of students, and what the student will be able to accomplish as an ultimate result. The school takes responsibility for the actions of staff and students alike, working to ensure that student and faculty peer cultures support the school's mission. Public high schools also try to give students valuable opportunities, but they do so diffidently, leaving it up to students to define per-

sonal goals and find the connection between school work and their future opportunities. In a public school, the faculty is obligated to provide instruction and
students are obligated to receive it. The neighborhood comprehensive public
school considers the student and faculty peer cultures noninstructional phenom-
ena, not intrinsic parts of its educational strategy.

Private voucher schools have a strong commitment to parenting and aggressively molding student attitudes and values. Because they are essentially collaborative enterprises, such schools must live by the secular ethics of reciprocity,
reliability, fairness, and respect for others. In contrast, public schools see themselves primarily as transmitters of information and imparters of skills. They do
not think it is appropriate to impose values and preferences on students; ethics is
a subject of study, not a set of principles that can be learned by the experience of
being in school.

Private voucher schools have centripetal curricula that draw all students
toward learning certain core skills and perspectives. The school's dedication to
preparing students for a certain kind of adult life means that the school must
work to ensure that all students master core subject matter; students cannot be
left behind because the teacher does not have time to explain a key point, and
no student may be relegated permanently to basic skills workbooks. Students who
enter with basic skills deficits are given special instruction and required to study
nights, summers, and weekends to catch up. Ultimately, however, they are all
exposed to the curriculum that the school defines as essential for all its graduates.
In contrast, public schools distinguish among students in terms of ability and
preference and offer profoundly different curricula to different groups. Many
students who would be drawn toward the core curriculum in a private voucher
school spend their entire high school careers in comprehensive school remedial
programs.

The Advantages of Choice

The Catholic schools that the private voucher recipients attended
enjoyed oganizational independence and benefited from the fact that all members of the school community could deal frankly and aggressively with one another. The schools, and the students in them, also drew major benefits from the
fact that students, parents, faculty, and staff had all chosen to be there. Partnership students, who were offered private vouchers virtually out of the blue, may
not have sought to attend Catholic schools but, by accepting the opportunity
once it was presented, they gained access to the advantages of choice.

Is choice itself valuable? Many members of the antichoice educational establishment claim that universal choice is of little value to the low-income and

minority students who now attend the worst schools. They say that low-income parents, not knowing the difference between good and bad schools, will make poor choices for their children and that vouchers, whether public or private, will be wasted.

The experience of Partnership students supports the contrary position, that mutual choice—between parents and schools and between schools and the teachers who work in them—is essential to educational success, particularly with disadvantaged students. This section shows how choice affects the motivations and performance of teachers, parents, and students and how it can make the difference between schools that are indifferent providers of routine academic courses and schools that are true communities and lead and develop students as whole people.

The evidence can be summarized under five propositions:

- The need to keep promises to parents makes the school's overall reputation of great importance to staff. This focuses their attention on instructional effectiveness first and all other issues second.

- Simply by choosing a school, parents convey an authority and legitimacy to the educational process that both motivates students and strengthens the school's ability to make demands.

- Parents do not have to choose innovative or unusual schools for these advantages to apply. Nor do parents need to be able to find a school they think is exactly right for their children. What matters is that parents consider the chosen school preferable to the available alternatives.

- Schools of choice can influence students' attitudes, motivation, and effort in ways that other schools cannot.

- A chosen school is far more likely than a nonchosen school to be a community in which students learn by example how adults in the real world live and work together.

HOW CHOICE AFFECTS SCHOOL STAFF

Schools that accept vouchers and other chosen schools need to attract students to survive. Although some can rely on a reputation for exclusivity or superior quality, not all schools can credibly claim to be better than all others. But every school can offer something—a specific curriculum, social climate, or extracurricular program—that gives it an identity and attracts the interest of parents and students. Once a school has established an identity, it must deliver on its promises so as to keep current students from transferring out, create "brand loyalty" among families with several children, and attract enough new families to fill the entering class each year.

The need for product differentiation encourages a number of behaviors that advocates of effective schools have tried to create. Teachers and principals in the private voucher schools have a strong incentive to articulate a mission for the school and to ensure that all elements of the school contribute to its attainment. The mission must also be easy to explain to parents, which means that it must focus on what children will experience in school and what they will be able to do on leaving it, not on subtleties of educational technique that may matter only to professionals.

Once a choice school has established an identity, the staff has a strong incentive—economic survival—to avoid major disruptions in the program and to be concerned about the performance of the school as a whole. If a school is forced to close because too few students want to attend it, all teachers have to find new jobs, no matter how well individual teachers taught their classes. Teachers therefore have strong incentives to keep their work in line with the school's mission, help one another, identify weaknesses, and ensure that variations in teacher performance do not harm the school's ultimate product and reputation.

All these behaviors are evident in the financially struggling nonelite religious schools attended by the Partnership students. Many staff members in such schools are eligible to work in regular public schools for equal or greater pay, but they stay in schools of choice out of commitment to the kind of education being offered in the school or because they prefer the working conditions. They therefore value their jobs, which they know would go away if the school were forced to close. Staff members know that their jobs depend on their own performance and that of their coworkers. They are therefore quick to seek advice from other teachers if a particular class is not going well and to alert their colleagues or the school management if another teacher is not pulling his weight. They are also reluctant to give up on a student, knowing that too many failure stories can wreck a school's reputation. Even when the student population changes, as a result of worsening economic conditions or demographic changes, teachers and administrators in schools of choice have strong incentives to maintain the level of student performance.

In contrast, staff members in neighboring public schools need not fear for their jobs if their school fails to perform. They are protected by civil service laws and union contracts, and as long as there are students in the neighborhood, they will have a job. Even if (as can happen in New York) the state intervenes to close a school, the teachers and administrators will be assigned to another school in the system. The school's reputation may be a source of pride, but people's livelihoods do not depend on it. Although most teachers want to do a good job, they are not driven by economic necessity to question their own performance or confront others who are not producing. Students who fail do not constitute a particular threat to the school. Staff members, knowing that serious self-assessment can lead to painful confrontations, have a strong incentive to explain declining student performance or rising dropout rates by telling themselves that the problem is with the students, not the school.

A small number of schools of choice have enough applicants that they can reject a student who shows signs of becoming an academic or behavior problem. But in a competitive situation, such as that faced by the New York City Catholic schools, schools of choice have no such luxury. Such schools must be, in Slavin's term, relentless in improving their own performance and helping students achieve. Contrary to the claims of the antichoice educational establishment, schools that serve private voucher students cannot survive by handpicking only exceptional students or by expelling any student who proves difficult to educate. They must, instead, work to keep students in school, influencing their students' attitudes and motivations as well as academic performance. Throughout the program's existence, Partnership students have been less likely than regular public school students to drop out or be involuntarily discharged: 24 percent of Partnership students quit or are asked to leave; the comparable figure for public high school students is 33 percent.

Staff members in the private voucher schools treat students as if they are educable, not frozen in either their academic abilities or their attitudes. This difference between schools of choice and assigned-attendance public schools is encapsulated in a sign displayed in a private school classroom: "Attitude is a decision you make."

HOW CHOICE AFFECTS PARENTS

Most of the literature promoting choice stresses the importance of making parents consumers, courted and respected by school staffs. As the preceding section shows, the possibility that parents will withdraw their children from a school of choice is a powerful motivator for teachers and principals and makes it possible for parents to intervene effectively if schools mistreat or neglect their children.

But as the experience of the private voucher schools shows, the connections between parents and schools of choice are more complex than a raw economic relationship. The choice of a school is more akin to the choice of a family doctor or pastor than to the choice of a car dealer or grocery store. The parent's status as a consumer is only the foundation of a much richer set of trust relationships between parent and child and child and school.

As Coleman has pointed out, a parent who chooses a school for her child gives the school a grant of parental authority. Even if the parent is simply responding to an opportunity offered by a charitable organization like the Partnership, she is free to say no and continue sending her child to the neighborhood public school. Parents choose for many reasons—educational taste, confidence in the school staff, fear of public school violence, or personal convenience. Once the parent has made a choice, the child knows that a change of school can upset and inconvenience the parent. Most children, not wanting to risk an upheaval at home, have a strong incentive to succeed in the school their parents have chosen for them.

By choosing, parents become part of the educational process. As one private voucher student said, "My mother says that I am lucky to be going to this school and I had better not mess up." Another said, "My uncle said [the public school the student previously attended] was no good but if I can't do good here there is something wrong with me." A student who skips school, does not study, or displays a sullen attitude is risking a parental confrontation. Although a few children will court such a confrontation, the vast majority will not. School staff are therefore able to use the parent's grant of authority to make demands on the student, saying, as one private voucher program principal did, "Your mother didn't send you here to hang out in the rest room. She sent you here to learn."

Chosen schools also have leverage with parents. The threat of rejection that motivates teachers and principals cuts both ways: the school can also decide not to continue educating a student. Once they have chosen a school and adjusted their transportation plans and schedules accordingly, parents do not like to make changes. Unless the school has failed to keep its part of the bargain, parents are reluctant to see their children's education disrupted. Schools of choice can, consequently, make demands on parents to monitor homework, ensure student attendance, and ensure that the student comes to school fed, rested, and ready to learn.

Although schools in the private voucher program understood that parents lacked the time and money to make donations, raise funds, or attend frequent meetings, they were direct and demanding about what parents must do if their children are to succeed in school. Private voucher schools found foster homes for students whose families were disrupted by death, unemployment, illness, or imprisonment. But they expected the family to support the educational process whenever it was physically possible.

Chosen schools' influence on parents is not all coercive; much of it is based on the parents' trust in the school's competence and concern for its students. Schools of choice, like family doctors, are influential because they are trusted. Patients follow their doctor's advice primarily because they expect to become healthier and only secondarily because they fear the doctor will refuse to see them again if they do not take the prescribed medicine. The same is true with families. The fact that parents have chosen a school, and that the school had an incentive to be as helpful as possible, creates a relationship of trust. Families that deal with the same school over a long time, especially those who have sent several children there, develop especially strong bonds of sentiment and loyalty toward the school.

Any trust relationship can be misused, and some schools of choice may retain parents' confidence longer than their performance merits. But in most cases the relationship creates major benefits for all parties. The private voucher schools felt confident in exhorting parents to become more important forces in their children's lives and to reinforce the school's opposition to the harmful elements of students' peer culture. One private voucher school principal required that parents attend only one meeting each year, before classes started in September, so that she could exhort parents to hold their children to traditional family standards, no matter how much children appeared to reject them.

A public school to which children are assigned because they are of school age and live in the neighborhood has no such grant of parental authority. On the contrary, teachers in public schools all over the country complain that "we can't teach these kids if their families don't care."

Choice affects the relationships between schools and parents even if the chosen school falls short of the parent's ideal. As long as the parent thinks the chosen school is better than any available alternative, the parent has reason to feel commitment to it. Schools need not be highly distinctive to get the benefit of a parent's choice. Even though educators may think low-cost parochial schools are similar, the parents who choose among them usually think the differences are important. The longer a family stays with a school, the more importance history and personal relationships assume.

Public schools can also build personal loyalties, and a parent whose children attend such a school can come to believe that it is just the right one. In such cases, the school probably gains an important grant of parental authority. But choice may play an important part even then. Higher-income parents, who always have the capacity to remove their children from attendance-zone schools, are the ones most likely to develop close relationships with teachers and administrators. Lower-income parents, who have little choice about where their children attend school, seldom develop strong feelings of confidence and loyalty. Parent advisory councils and other mechanisms for parent involvement in school governance only influence the few parents who participate.

As the private voucher program experience shows, however, choice gives low-income parents the same sense of commitment and loyalty that higher-income parents enjoy. The schools' religious identity obviously builds some trust. But the fact that the parents have been able to accept or reject the Partnership's tuition grant creates a sense of mutual commitment between parent and school.

HOW CHOICE AFFECTS STUDENTS

Many of choice's effects on students are implicit in the foregoing. Students in schools of choice benefit from teachers' and principals' need to create a defined image and reputation. Students also benefit from their parents' commitment to the school and from the school's consequent ability to make demands on their parents and themselves.

Beyond these advantages, students derive two other benefits from being in schools of choice. First, they gain from being in a situation where they themselves must make commitments and take them seriously. Second, they gain from observing adults working in a common enterprise where performance matters and both success and failure have real consequences.

Value of Student Commitment. Students may prefer not to attend any school at all, as may have been the case with many private voucher students. But if a student has any preference for the school she now attends over other schools she might have to attend if she fails in the current one, she is susceptible to influence. This is true even if the school preference is based on nonacademic factors such as location, sports teams, or presence of friends. It is especially important if students have knowingly chosen a school that offers a particular academic emphasis or makes special demands on effort and performance. When students make such a commitment, they implicitly admit that the chosen school is more attractive than the alternatives. The possibility that the chosen school will reject them if they fail to meet its demands is a strong motivation for effort. Although they may prefer not to do all the school requires, they know that failing to do so could result in their being forced to leave the chosen school and go to another that is less attractive to them.

Students in the Partnership schools frankly admitted that they had made a trade-off in accepting a private voucher. All knew that leaving public school would separate them from friends and neighborhood and would subject them to firm demands about attendance and academic effort. They accepted the Partnership's offer of free tuition for many reasons—because the private schools were safer, because they hoped (along with virtually all high school students) someday to attend college, or because they liked the schools' traditions and sports teams. But they all understood what the schools would demand of them because the school admissions counselors and the Partnership program itself made sure that they knew.

Once they accepted the schools' demands, they had given the schools leverage: teachers and administrators could assign homework, take attendance, grade performance, and administer consequences just as they had said they would. Armed with this authority, the private voucher schools exercised their authority confidently—not in a harsh or morally superior way but matter-of-factly, as the simple consequence of a well-understood bargain.

Less than 10 percent of the students offered scholarships rejected them. Once students accepted the Partnership's offer, the vast majority understood the bargain they had made and accepted, albeit grudgingly, the schools' rigorous execution of it. Students understood the consequence of failing to fulfill their part of the bargain. They were also susceptible to the schools' use of cognitive dissonance. When students failed to complete assigned work or broke school rules, teachers consistently said, "You made an agreement when you came here, now live up to it." For the vast majority of students, the need to uphold a commitment both influenced their behavior and changed their attitudes. In surveys and interviews, virtually all students said that their effort, attendance, and attitudes about schooling had all changed since they joined the Partnership program.

Emulation of Adult Working Relationships. During the fieldwork for *High Schools with Character,* and in subsequent work in urban high schools, the RAND research team observed the operation of a hidden curriculum, which schools taught by example, not didactically. That example is provided by teachers and administrators, the only adults whom students routinely see at work. It can send a powerful message to students, that the work of adults requires clear goals, collaborative effort, initiative, reciprocity, and risk taking.

As Carl Glickman (1993) and others confirm, teachers in public schools often feel that they have little control over the conditions of their own work and think that they and their colleagues are neither rewarded for diligence nor punished for negligence. For adults in such situations the rational response is to do exactly what their formal job description requires and not to take responsibility for the overall product of the organization in which they work. Albert Shanker's quote from an urban teacher, "I taught them but they didn't learn it," encapsulates the phenomenon. Many teachers and administrators in public schools think differently, but they are not rewarded by the organization or, in many cases, appreciated by their coworkers. For students, who seldom observe any adults other than teachers at work, the message can be powerful: large organizations that employ adults do not have clear goals and do not require or support effective work.

The hidden curriculum in schools of choice is different. The adults in private voucher schools were not necessarily more virtuous than teachers and administrators elsewhere, but because they were linked in a common enterprise, they had incentives to work together and hold one another accountable. The version of adult life and responsibility modeled in such schools is very different from that in schools that lack a clear mission and in which staff members do not have to perform to keep their jobs. The message to students in choice schools is that adults depend on and influence one another and care about whether they and others are contributing to the success of a broader enterprise.

Students get the message. One student interviewed in a public school sharply echoed other students: "Nobody here does any more than you have to do. I'm not going to be a chump." Students in private voucher schools, in contrast, saw how hard faculty members worked to make the school succeed. As one private voucher student who had recently transferred from public school said, "In public school the teachers say, 'I get paid whether you learn this or not.' Here, they say, 'You are going to learn this if it takes all day. I don't care how long it takes: I live upstairs.'"

It does not take a private or religious school to teach these lessons. Many of the nonselective magnet schools studied by Crain (1992) and for *High Schools with Character* provide similar examples of earnest adult collaboration. There are, furthermore, many teachers and administrators in nonchosen public schools who provide sterling personal examples. But those individuals are forced to overcome the context in which they work, whereas teachers and administrators in schools of choice are reinforced by everything about their working environment.

Conclusion

Private vouchers give low-income students access to schools that are strong because they are institutionally independent and effective because everyone in them is there by choice. Schools that students can attend with private vouchers are profoundly different as educational environments from regular public schools. Even when their academic offerings are not much different from those of public schools, schools of choice provide an environment in which parents and teachers are collaborators, bargains among adults and between adults and children are made and kept, effort is rewarded, and actions have consequences. Such environments motivate student effort in the short run. In the longer run, they socialize students into the values and attitudes required in adult life.

The charter schools movement and school reform networks led by Ted Sizer of Brown, Henry Levin of Stanford, James Comer of Yale, and others hope to increase the numbers of public schools with the attributes listed above. Doing so will require a profound change in the mission and operation of public schools. It surely requires choice—school choice of teachers, student and parent choice of schools, and choice about how long to stick with a student who will not fulfill the school's work requirements. Some (e.g., Chubb and Moe 1992) think that a universal system of public vouchers or scholarships would naturally elicit a supply of good schools. Others, the present author included, think that marketlike mechanisms are indispensable but that reform of public education also requires an effort by public authorities to attract new providers into public education by offering charters and contracts to public agencies, teacher groups, nonprofit organizations, and private profit-making firms (see, for example, Hill 1994).

Such public sector reforms face strong opposition from teacher unions and school administrator groups. Even if opposition can be overcome, it will take a long time to create a new supply of strong public schools, especially in inner-city areas where most public schools are now weak and poorly staffed. In the short run (i.e., any time before the year 2000), vouchers that allow students to attend existing private schools are the only sure way to guarantee that large numbers of low-income and minority students get the educational advantages of choice. Unlike charter schools and public magnet schools, private vouchers can be targeted exclusively to the most needy. They cannot be hijacked by aggressive middle-class parents or diluted by legislators who want to spread the benefits as widely as possible. Private vouchers can also help save a major American cultural resource, the nonselective low-cost private school.

The public education system needs to be reformed from the ground up. Private vouchers cannot do that; there is not enough money in private hands, and there are too few private schools to serve every student who is stuck in a bad public school. But private voucher programs such as the Student-Sponsor Partnership Program can preserve a precious national resource, the low-cost church-sponsored school, and rescue the neediest students from the worst problems of today's public schools.

References

Bryk, Anthony C., and Valerie Lee. 1993. *Catholic schools and the common good.* Cambridge, Mass.: Harvard University Press.

Chubb, John E. and Terry M. Moe. 1992. *Politics, markets, and America's schools.* Washington, D.C.: Brookings Institution.

City of New York, Office of the Comptroller. 1993. *Half the battle: The high school dropout rate is down, but the graduation rate is not rising.* New York: Office of Policy Management.

Coleman, James S., Thomas Hoffer, and Sally Kilgore. 1982. *High school achievement: Public, Catholic, and private schools compared.* New York: Basic Books.

Crain, Robert, et al. 1992. *The effectiveness of New York City's career magnets.* Berkeley, Calif.: National Center for Research on Vocational Education.

Glickman, Carl D. 1993. *Renewing America's schools: A guide for school-based action.* San Francisco: Jossey-Bass.

Hill, Paul T. 1991. *High schools with character.* Santa Monica, Calif.: RAND.

———. 1995. *Reinventing public education.* Santa Monica, Calif.: RAND.